MENARDS® Vacation & Small HOME PLANS

Vacation & Small Home Plans

Vacation & Small Home Plans is a collection of our best-selling vacation and small homes in a variety of styles. These plans cover a wide range of architectural styles. A broad assortment is presented to match a wide variety of lifestyles and budgets. Each plan page features floor plans, a front view of the house, interior square footage of the home, number of bedrooms, baths, garage size and foundation types. All floor plans show room and exterior dimensions.

Technical Specifications

At the time the construction drawings were prepared, every effort was made to ensure that these plans and specifications meet nationally recognized building codes (BOCA, Southern Building Code Congress and others). Because national building codes change or vary from area to area some drawing modifications and/or the assistance of a professional designer or architect may be necessary to comply with your local codes or to accommodate specific building site conditions. We advise you to consult with your local building official for information regarding codes governing your area.

Blueprint Ordering - Fast & Easy

Your ordering is made simple by following the instructions on page 7. See page 6 for more information on which types of blueprint packages are available and how many plan sets to order.

Your Home, Your Way

The blueprints you receive are a master plan for building your new home. They start you on your way to what may well be the most rewarding experience of your life.

Current printing 5 4 3 2

VACATION & SMALL HOME PLANS is published by HDA, Inc., 944 Anglum Road, St. Louis, MO, 63042. All rights reserved. Reproduction in whole or in part without written permission of the publisher is prohibited. Printed in U.S.A. © 2012.

Artist drawings and photos shown in this publication may vary slightly from the actual working drawings. Some photos are shown in mirror reverse. Please refer to the floor plan for accurate layout.

Contents

COVER HOME The house shown on the front cover is plan #M07-007D-0060 and is featured on page 18. Photo courtesy of HDA, Inc.

COVER HOME The house shown on the front cover is plan #M07-055L-0526 and is featured on page 97. Photo courtesy of Nelson Design Group.

COVER HOME The house shown on the front cover is plan #M07-072L-0013 and is featured on page 21. Photo courtesy of Lifestyle Home Design.

Let **MENARDS** *Make Your Dream Home A Reality*

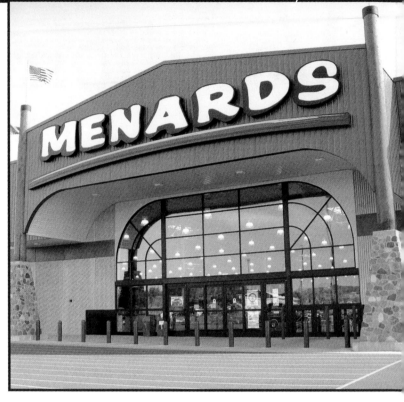

"Thanks to **MENARDS**, *finding and building our Dream Home has never been easier."*

Thinking about building your dream home? Or, perhaps you are interested in a vacation home or downsizing to a smaller home? Choosing a home plan can be a daunting task.

This book of Vacation & Small Home Plans has been designed to make the search simple and easy. Browse the pages of this book and look for the style that best suits your family and your needs. These plans have been chosen from top designers from across the country and can provide to you the perfect home that will truly be a place of refuge for your whole family for years to come.

This book is the perfect place to begin your search for the home of your dreams. You will find the expected beauty you want and the functional efficiency you need, all designed with unmatched quality.

Also, keep in mind, this book contains helpful articles for understanding what kind of plan package you may need as well as other helpful building aids to make the process even easier. When you have made this decision visit your local **MENARDS** store to place your order and partner with one of their friendly team members to walk you through the process or order your home plans at www.Menards.com.

MENARDS is dedicated to assist you through the entire home decision process

Choosing a home plan is an exciting but difficult task. Many factors play a role in what home plan is best for you and your family. To help you get started, we have pinpointed some of the major factors to consider when searching for your dream home. Take the time to evaluate your family's needs and you will have an easier time sorting through all of the home plans offered in our magazine.

Budget: The first thing to consider is your budget. Many items take part in this budget, from ordering the blueprints to the last doorknob purchased. When you find your dream home plan, visit the **MENARDS®** Building Materials Desk to get a cost-to-build estimate to ensure that the finished product will be within your cost range.

Family Lifestyle: After your budget is deciphered, you need to assess you and your family's lifestyle needs. Think about the stage of life you are at now, and what stages you will be going through in the future. Ask yourself questions to figure out how much room you need now and if you will need room for expansion. Are you married? Do you have children? How many children do you plan on having? Are you an empty-nester?

Incorporate in your planning any frequent guests you may have, including elderly parents, grandchildren or adult children who may live with you.

Does your family entertain a lot? If so, think about the rooms you will need to do so. Will you need both formal and informal spaces? Do you need a gourmet kitchen? Do you need a game room and/or a wet bar?

Experts in the field suggest that the best way to determine your needs is to begin by listing everything you like or dislike about your current home.

Floor Plan Layouts: When looking through our home plans, imagine yourself walking through the house. Consider the flow from the entry to the living, sleeping and gathering areas. Does the layout ensure privacy for the master bedroom? Does the garage enter near the kitchen for easy unloading? Does the placement of the windows provide enough privacy from any neighboring properties? Do you plan on using furniture you already have? Will this furniture fit in the appropriate rooms? When you find a plan you want to purchase, be sure to picture yourself actually living in it.

Exterior Spaces: There are many different home styles ranging from Traditional to Contemporary. Flip through and find which style most appeals to you and the neighborhood in which you plan to build. Also think of your site and how the entire house will fit on this site. Picture any landscaping you plan on incorporating into the design. Using your imagination is key when choosing a home plan.

Choosing a home plan can be an intimidating experience. Asking yourself these questions before you get started on the search will help you through the process. With our large selection of multiple styles we are certain you will find your dream home in the following pages.

Our Blueprint Packages Offer...

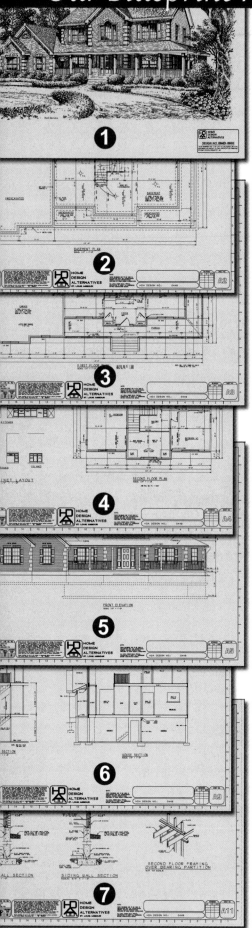

*Quality plans for building your future,
with extras that provide unsurpassed value,
ensure good construction and long-term enjoyment.*

A quality home - one that looks good, functions well, and provides years of enjoyment - is a product of many things - design, materials, and craftsmanship.

But it's also the result of outstanding blueprints - the actual plans and specifications that tell the builder exactly how to build your home.

And with our BLUEPRINT PACKAGES you get the absolute best.
A complete set of blueprints is available for every design in this book.
These "working drawings" are highly detailed, resulting in two key benefits:

- Better understanding by the contractor of how to build your home and...

- More accurate construction estimates.

Below is a sample of plan information included for most of the designs in this book. Specific details may vary with each designer's plan.

1. Cover Sheet is the artist's rendering of the exterior of the home and is included with many of the plans. It will give you an idea of how your home will look when completed and landscaped.

2. Foundation plan shows the layout of the basement, crawl space, slab or pier foundation. All necessary notations and dimensions are included. See the plan page for the foundation types included. If the home plan you choose does not have your desired foundation type, see page 8 on how to customize your foundation to suit your specific needs or site conditions.

3. Floor Plans show the placement of walls, doors, closets, plumbing fixtures, electrical outlets, columns, and beams for each level of the home.

4. Interior Elevations provide views of special interior elements such as fireplaces, kitchen cabinets, built-in units and other features of the home.

5. Exterior Elevations illustrate the front, rear and both sides of the house, with all details of exterior materials and the required dimensions.

6. Sections show detail views of the home or portions of the home as if it were sliced from the roof to the foundation. This sheet shows important areas such as load-bearing walls, stairs, joists, trusses and other structural elements, which are critical for proper construction.

7. Details show how to construct certain components of your home, such as the roof system, stairs, deck, etc.

The Legal Kit™

Home building can be a complicated process with many legal regulations being confusing. This Legal Kit was designed to help you avoid many legal pitfalls and build your home with confidence using the forms and contracts featured in this kit. Included are request for proposal documents, various fixed price and cost plus contracts, instructions on how and when to use each form, warranty statements and more. Save time and money before you break ground on your new home or start a remodeling project. Instructions are included on how to use the kit and since the documents are universal, they are designed to be used with all building trades. Since review by an attorney is always advised before signing any contract, this is an ideal way to get organized and started on the process. Plus, all forms are reproducible making it a terrific tool for the contractor and home builder.

Discount Price: $35.00 - Menards SKU 100-3422

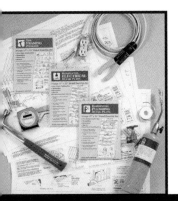

Detail Plan Packages

Framing, Plumbing and Electrical Plan Packages

Three separate packages offer home builders details for constructing various foundations; numerous floor, wall and roof framing techniques; simple to complex residential wiring; sump and water softener hookups; plumbing connection methods; installation of septic systems, and more. Packages include 3-dimensional illustrations and a glossary of terms. These drawings do not pertain to a specific home plan making them perfect for your building situation. Purchase one or all three.

Discount Price: $20.00 each or all three for $40.00 - Menards SKU 100-3422

Your Blueprint Package will contain the necessary construction information to build your home. We also offer the following products and services to save you time and money in the building process.

Express Delivery

Most orders are processed within 24 hours of receipt. Please allow 7-10 business days for delivery. If you need to place a rush order, please call or visit any **MENARDS**®store to order by 11:00 a.m. Monday-Friday CST and specify you would like express service (allow 1-2 business days).

Discount Price: $50.00 - Menards SKU 194-4356

Technical Assistance

If you have questions, call our technical support line at 1-314-770-2228 Monday through Friday, 8am-5pm CST. Whether it involves design modifications or field assistance, our designers are extremely familiar with all of our designs and will be happy to help you. We want your home to be everything you expect it to be.

Material List

Material lists are available for all of the plans in this book. Each list gives you the quantity, dimensions and description of the building materials necessary to construct your home. You'll get faster and more accurate bids from your contractor while saving money by paying for only the materials you need. To receive a free home plan estimate call or visit any **MENARDS**® Building Materials Desk.

Discount Price: $125.00 - Menards SKU 100-3422

NOTE: Material lists are not refundable. A material list can only be sold when at least one set of blueprints has been purchased. They cannot be purchased separately. Material lists are designed with the standard foundation only and will not include alternate or optional foundations.

What Kind Of Plan Package Do You Need?

Now that you've found the home you've been looking for, here are some suggestions on how to make your Dream Home a reality. To get started, order the type of plans that fit your particular situation.

Your Choices

☐ **The One-Set Study Package** - We offer a One-set plan package so you can study your home in detail. This one set is considered a study set and is marked "not for construction." It is a copyright violation to reproduce blueprints.

☐ **The Minimum 5-Set Package** - If you're ready to start the construction process, this 5-set package is the minimum number of blueprint sets you will need. It will require keeping close track of each set so they can be used by multiple subcontractors and tradespeople.

☐ **The Standard 8-Set Package** - For best results in terms of cost, schedule and quality of construction, we recommend you order eight (or more) sets of blueprints. Besides one set for yourself, additional sets of blueprints will be required by your mortgage lender, local building department, general contractor and all subcontractors working on foundation, electrical, plumbing, heating/air conditioning, carpentry work, etc.

☐ **Reproducible Masters** - If you wish to make some minor design changes, you'll want to order reproducible masters. These drawings contain the same information as the blueprints but are printed on reproducible paper and clearly indicates your right to alter, copy or reproduce. This will allow your builder or a local design professional to make the necessary drawing changes without the major expense of redrawing the plans. This package also allows you to print copies of the modified plans as needed. The right of building only one structure from these plans is licensed exclusively to the buyer. You may not use this design to build a second or multiple dwelling(s) without purchasing another blueprint. Each violation of the Copyright Law is punishable in a fine.

☐ **Mirror Reverse Sets** - Plans can be printed in mirror reverse. These plans are useful when the house would fit your site better if all the rooms were on the opposite side than shown. They are simply a mirror image of the original drawings causing the lettering and dimensions to read backwards. Therefore, when ordering mirror reverse drawings, you must purchase at least one set of right-reading plans. Some of our plans are offered mirror reverse right-reading. This means the plan, lettering and dimensions are flipped but read correctly. Right reading reverse is not available for all plans. See the Home Plan Index on page 224 for availability.

☐ **Right Reading Reverse Sets** - Right reading reverse is where the plan is a mirrored image of the original drawings, but all the text and dimensions read correctly. This option may not be available for all home plans, so please check the Home Plan Index on page 224 for availability.

☐ **Additional Sets** - Additional sets of the plan ordered are available for an additional cost of $45.00 each. Five-set, eight-set, and reproducible packages offer considerable savings. *Note: Available only within 90 days after purchase of plan package or reproducible masters of the same plan.*

You've found your Dream Home, now what?

Follow these simple steps:

1. Review the article on page 6 to decide what type of plan package you need.

2. To order, call or visit any **MENARDS®** store and go to the Building Materials Desk or visit **www.Menards.com**.

To locate the **MENARDS®** store nearest you, go to **www.Menards.com**, then click on the Store locator.

Artist drawings and photos shown in this publication may vary slightly from the actual working drawings. Some photos are shown in mirror reverse. Please refer to the floor plan for accurate layout.

Blueprint SKU Pricing
(prices subject to change)

PRICE CODE		1-SET STUDY	5-SET PLAN	8-SET PLAN	REPRO. MASTERS
AAA	Menards SKU	194-3920	194-3933	194-3946	194-3959
	Discount Price	$310	$410	$510	$610
AA	Menards SKU	194-3962	194-3975	194-3988	194-3991
	Discount Price	$410	$510	$610	$710
A	Menards SKU	194-4000	194-4084	194-4165	194-4246
	Discount Price	$470	$570	$670	$770
B	Menards SKU	194-4013	194-4097	194-4178	194-4259
	Discount Price	$530	$630	$730	$830
C	Menards SKU	194-4026	194-4107	194-4181	194-4262
	Discount Price	$585	$685	$785	$885
D	Menards SKU	194-4039	194-4110	194-4194	194-4275
	Discount Price	$635	$735	$835	$935
E	Menards SKU	194-4042	194-4123	194-4204	194-4288
	Discount Price	$695	$795	$895	$995
F	Menards SKU	194-4055	194-4136	194-4217	194-4291
	Discount Price	$750	$850	$950	$1050
G	Menards SKU	194-4068	194-4149	194-4220	194-4301
	Discount Price	$1000	$1100	$1200	$1300
H	Menards SKU	194-4071	194-4152	194-4233	194-4314
	Discount Price	$1100	$1200	$1300	$1400

OTHER PRODUCTS & BUILDING AIDS

MIRROR REVERSE*
Menards SKU   194-4327
Discount Price $15

RIGHT READING REVERSE*
Menards SKU   194-4328
Discount Price $150

ADDITIONAL SETS**
Menards SKU   194-4330
Discount Price $45

MATERIAL LIST**
Menards SKU   100-3422
Discount Price $125

EXPRESS DELIVERY
Menards SKU   194-4356
Discount Price $50

LEGAL KIT
Menards SKU   100-3422
Discount Price $35

DETAIL PLAN PACKAGES
ELECTRICAL, PLUMBING & FRAMING - ALL SAME SKU
Menards SKU   100-3422
Discount Price $20 EA.
3 FOR $40

If at any time you feel you may need assistance in the field while building, HDA offers a technical assistance line for answering building questions pertaining to your specific plan. Please call 314-770-2228 Monday-Friday between 8:00am and 5:00pm CST and our professional design staff will be happy to help.

Please note: All blueprints are printed in response to your order, so we cannot honor requests for refunds. However, if for some reason you find that the plan you have purchased does not meet your requirements, you may exchange that plan for another plan in our collection within 90 days of purchase. At the time of the exchange, you will be charged a processing fee of 25% of your original plan package price, plus the difference in price between the plan packages (if applicable) and the cost to ship the new plans to you. Keep in mind, reproducible drawings can only be exchanged if the package is unopened and material lists can only be purchased within 90 days of purchasing the plan package.

*See page 6
**Available only within 90 days after purchase of plan package of same plan

We understand that it is difficult to find blueprints that will meet all your needs. That is why HDA, Inc. is pleased to offer plan modification services.

Thinking About Customizing Your Plan?

If you're like many customers, you may want to make changes to your home plan to make it the dream home you've always wanted. That's where our expert design and modification team comes in. You won't find a more efficient and economic way to get your changes done than by using our design services.

Whether it's enlarging a kitchen, adding a porch or converting a crawl space to a basement, we can customize any plan and make it perfect for your family. Simply create your wish list and let us go to work. Soon you'll have the blueprints for your new home and at a fraction of the cost of hiring an architect!

The HDA Modification Advantage

- We can customize any of the thousands of plans
- FREE cost estimates for your home plan modifications within 48 hours (Monday-Friday, 8am-5pm CST).
- Average turn-around time to complete the modifications is 2-3 weeks.
- One-on-one design consultations.

Easy Steps For Fast Service

Visit any MENARDS® Building Materials Desk and request an HDA Custom Change Form.

Simply follow the instructions to receive your quote within two business days.

Customizing Facts

- The average cost for us to customize a house plan is typically less than 1 percent of the building costs — compare that to the national average of 7 percent of building costs.
- The average modification cost for a home is typically $800 to $1,500 (this does not include the cost of the reproducible blueprint, which is required to make plan changes).
- The average cost to modify a project plan is typically between $200-$500.

Other Helpful Information

- Feel free to include a sketch, or a specific list of changes you'd like to make.
- One of our designers will contact you within 24 hours with your free estimate.
- Upon accepting the estimate, you will need to purchase the reproducible set of plans.
- A contract, which includes a specific list of changes and fees will be sent to you for approval.
- Upon approving the contract, our designers will keep you up to date by emailing or faxing sketches throughout the project.
- Plan can be converted to metric.
- Barrier Free Conversion (accommodating a plan for special needs, transferring your living space for everyone).
- Customizing is also available for project plans, such as sheds, garages, apartment garages and more.

MENARDS®
Vacation & Small
HOME PLANS

Plan #M07-058D-0078 on page 20.

The following pages include a collection of best-selling home plans featuring vacation and small homes that are designed for efficient and easy living. This collection of homes from some of the nation's leading designers and architects include functional floor plans, abundant storage, and many designed perfectly for narrow lots. Whether you're interested in a cozy bungalow or compact two-story, these small homes will welcome you and create the perfect atmosphere for quality family living in an enjoyable setting. We are excited to present this collection designed for functional living. Whatever your tastes or needs, we invite you to discover the home of your dreams.

Plan #M07-022D-0014 on page 16.

Plan #M07-072L-0024 on page 27.

Prestbury

Plan #M07-055L-0289

Photo, above - The stylish kitchen maintains a compact floor plan, perfect for high function while it is only steps away from the great room and dining room.

Photo, left - This home highlights the kitchen with many of the most popular interior spaces surrounding it.

Photo, above - Stylish and sophisticated, the private master bath has a unique separate shower with sleek style. An oversized garden tub is sure to relieve stress for the homeowners in the private and amenity-filled master bath.

Photo, right - This homeowner moved the fireplace to act as a natural partition between the great room and the formal dining room. Arched entryways flank the see-through fireplace while providing a bold symmetrical design element.

Plan #M07-055L-0289

Lavishing Southern Design

1,504 total square feet of living area

3 bedrooms, 2 baths

2-car garage

Crawl space or slab foundation, please specify when ordering

Special features

A private master suite has its own luxury bath featuring an oversized tub and shower

A full bath is positioned between the two secondary bedrooms for convenience

Enjoy the outdoors on the covered porch directly off the breakfast room

Price Code C

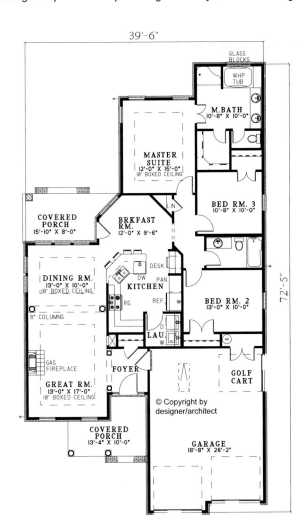

To order this plan, visit the Menards Building Materials Desk or visit www.Menards.com.

11

Plan #M07-077L-0097

Photo, above - Clean and effortless, the style of the great room is the perfect balance of formal and informal touches.

Photo, left - This angle of the kitchen shows off the stylish symmetry of the cabinetry and the center island work space.

Photo, above - Right off the foyer is a flex space that has been adapted here to a formal dining room with elegant chair rail details circumferencing the entire room.

Photo, right - Just one fine detail of the master bath, this sunk-in tub is the perfect place to rinse away the day.

Plan #M07-077L-0097

Beautiful Brick And Siding Combination

1,800 total square feet of living area

3 bedrooms, 2 baths

2-car side entry garage

Slab, basement or crawl space foundation, please specify when ordering

Special features

Double doors open into the foyer crowned with a 10' ceiling

The vaulted great room opens into the kitchen and bayed breakfast area with decorative columns

The unfinished bonus room has an additional 302 square feet of living area

Price Code D

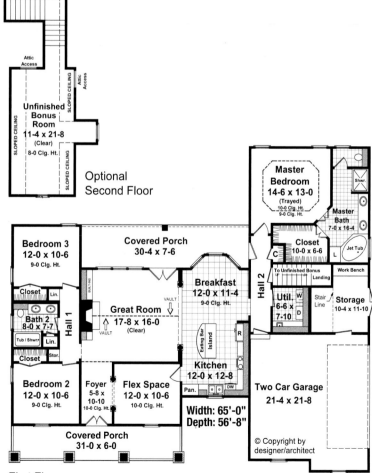

Optional Second Floor

Unfinished Bonus Room 11-4 x 21-8 (Clear) 8-0 Clg. Ht.

First Floor
1,800 sq. ft.

Bedroom 3 12-0 x 10-6 9-0 Clg. Ht.

Covered Porch 30-4 x 7-6

Master Bedroom 14-6 x 13-0 (Trayed) 10-0 Clg. Ht. 9-0 Clg. Ht.

Master Bath 7-0 x 16-4

Closet 10-0 x 6-6

Breakfast 12-0 x 11-4 9-0 Clg. Ht.

Great Room 17-8 x 16-0 (Clear)

Bath 2 8-0 x 7-7

Util. 6-6 x 7-10

Storage 10-4 x 11-10

Work Bench

Bedroom 2 12-0 x 10-6 9-0 Clg. Ht.

Foyer 5-8 x 10-10 10-0 Clg. Ht.

Flex Space 12-0 x 10-6 10-0 Clg. Ht.

Kitchen 12-0 x 12-8

Two Car Garage 21-4 x 21-8

Width: 65'-0"
Depth: 56'-8"

© Copyright by designer/architect

Covered Porch 31-0 x 6-0

To order this plan, visit the Menards Building Materials Desk or visit www.Menards.com.

13

Concord

MENARDS

Plan #M07-041D-0006

Spacious Vaulted Great Room

1,189 total square feet of living area

3 bedrooms, 2 1/2 baths

2-car garage

Basement foundation

Special features

All bedrooms are located on the second floor for added privacy

The dining room and kitchen both have views of the patio

The convenient half bath is located near the kitchen

The master bedroom has a private bath

Price Code AA

Rear View

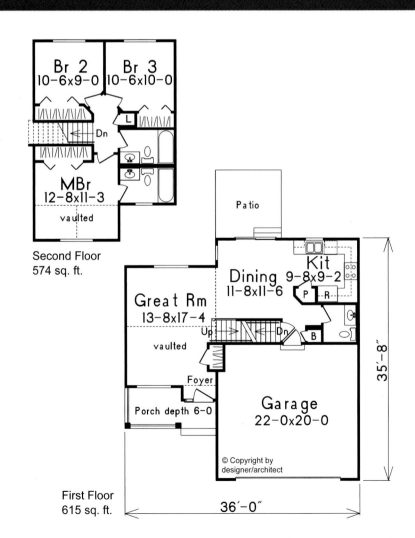

Br 2
10-6x9-0

Br 3
10-6x10-0

Dn

MBr
12-8x11-3
vaulted

Second Floor
574 sq. ft.

Patio

Kit
9-8x9-2

Dining
11-8x11-6

Great Rm
13-8x17-4
vaulted

Up   Dn

Foyer

Porch depth 6-0

Garage
22-0x20-0

© Copyright by
designer/architect

35'-8"

36'-0"

First Floor
615 sq. ft.

To order this plan, visit the Menards Building Materials Desk or visit www.Menards.com.

Ashley Park

Plan #M07-007D-0054

Second Floor
773 sq. ft.

First Floor
802 sq. ft.

© Copyright by designer/architect

Stylish Living For A Narrow Lot

1,575 total square feet of living area

3 bedrooms, 2 1/2 baths

2-car garage

Basement foundation, drawings also include crawl space and slab foundations

Special features

The kitchen with corner windows features an island snack bar, attractive breakfast room bay, convenient laundry area and built-in pantry

A luxury bath and walk-in closet adorn the master bedroom suite

Price Code B

Rear View

To order this plan, visit the Menards Building Materials Desk or visit www.Menards.com.

15

Treebrooke

MENARDS

Plan #M07-022D-0014

Country Kitchen Is Center Of Living Activities

1,556 total square feet of living area

3 bedrooms, 2 1/2 baths

2-car garage

Basement foundation

Special features

A compact home with all the amenities

The country kitchen combines practicality with access to other areas for eating and entertaining

A three-way fireplace joins the dining and living areas

A plant shelf and vaulted ceiling highlight the master bedroom

Price Code B

Rear View

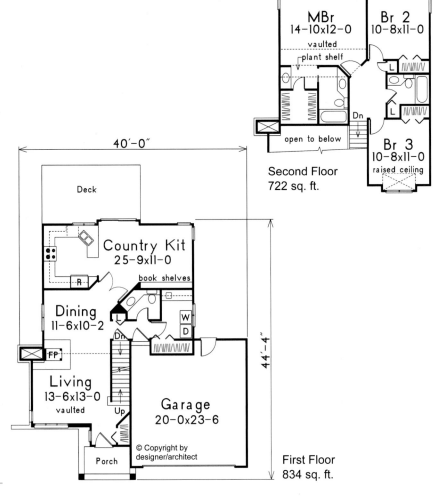

Second Floor
722 sq. ft.

MBr
14-10x12-0
vaulted
plant shelf

Br 2
10-8x11-0

open to below

Dn

Br 3
10-8x11-0
raised ceiling

40'-0"

Deck

Country Kit
25-9x11-0
book shelves

R

Dining
11-6x10-2

W
D

Dn

FP

Living
13-6x13-0
vaulted

Up

Garage
20-0x23-6

44'-4"

© Copyright by designer/architect

Porch

First Floor
834 sq. ft.

To order this plan, visit the Menards Building Materials Desk or visit www.Menards.com.

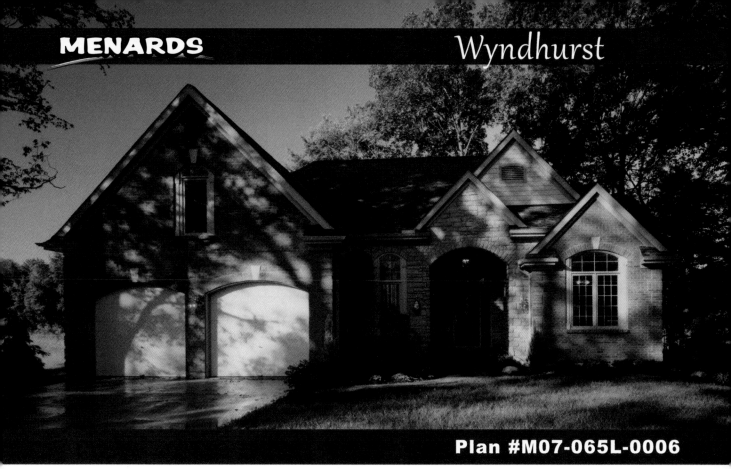

Plan #M07-065L-0006

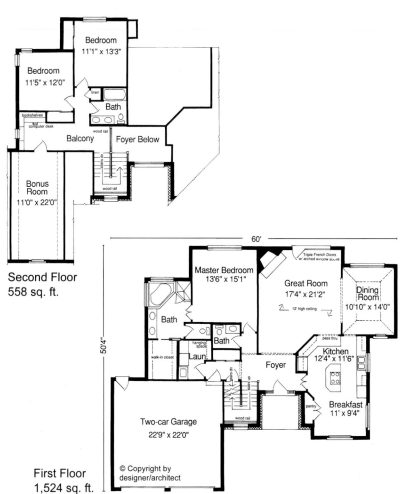

Bedroom
11'1" x 13'3"

Bedroom
11'5" x 12'0"

linen

Bath

bookshelves
computer desk

Balcony   Foyer Below

wood rail

Bonus
Room
11'0" x 22'0"

wood rail

Second Floor
558 sq. ft.

60'

Master Bedroom
13'6" x 15'1"

Triple French Doors
w/ arched window above

Great Room
17'4" x 21'2"

12' high ceiling

Dining
Room
10'10" x 14'0"

Bath

50'4"

Bath

hanging space

pass thru

walk-in closet

Laun

Kitchen
12'4" x 11'6"

Foyer

stairs up / stairs dn

pantry

Breakfast
11' x 9'4"

Two-car Garage
22'9" x 22'0"

wood rail

© Copyright by
designer/architect

First Floor
1,524 sq. ft.

Computer Area Is A Handy Feature

2,082 total square feet of living area

3 bedrooms, 2 1/2 baths

2-car garage

Basement foundation

Special features

This home is designed with an insulated foundation system featuring pre-mounted insulation on concrete walls providing a drier, warmer and smarter structure

The master bedroom boasts a deluxe bath and a large walk-in closet

Natural light floods the breakfast room through numerous windows

The great room features a 12' ceiling, cozy fireplace and stylish French doors

Bonus room on the second floor has an additional 267 square feet of living area

Price Code C

To order this plan, visit the *Menards Building Materials Desk* or visit www.Menards.com.

17

Ashmont

Plan #M07-007D-0060

Distinguished Styling
For A Small Lot

1,268 total square feet of living area

3 bedrooms, 2 baths

2-car garage

Basement foundation, drawings also include crawl space and slab foundations

Special features

Multiple gables, a large porch and arched windows create a classy exterior

Innovative design provides openness in the great room, kitchen and breakfast area

The secondary bedrooms have a private hall with bath

2" x 6" exterior walls available, please order plan #M07-007E-0060

Price Code B

Rear View

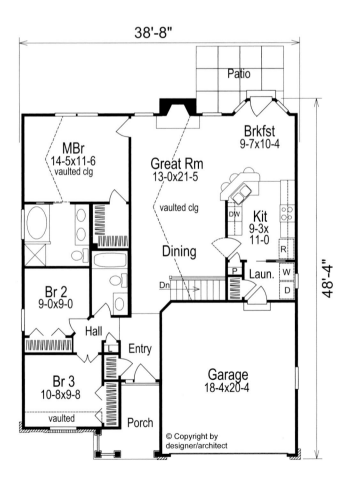

38'-8"

Patio

MBr
14-5x11-6
vaulted clg

Great Rm
13-0x21-5

vaulted clg

Brkfst
9-7x10-4

Kit
9-3x
11-0

DW

Dining

Br 2
9-0x9-0

Dn

P   Laun.

W
D

Hall

Entry

Br 3
10-8x9-8

vaulted

Porch

Garage
18-4x20-4

48'-4"

© Copyright by
designer/architect

To order this plan, visit the Menards Building Materials Desk or visit www.Menards.com.

Plan #M07-027D-0005

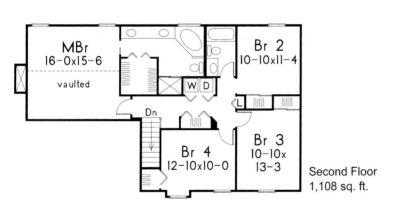

Second Floor
1,108 sq. ft.

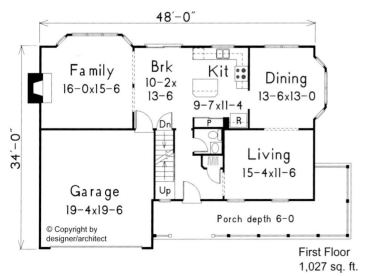

First Floor
1,027 sq. ft.

Open Breakfast/Family Room Combination

2,135 total square feet of living area

4 bedrooms, 2 1/2 baths

2-car garage

Basement foundation

Special features

The family room features extra space, an impressive fireplace and full wall of windows that joins the breakfast area creating a spacious entertainment area

The washer and dryer are conveniently located on the second floor near the bedrooms

The kitchen features an island counter and pantry

Price Code D

Rear View

To order this plan, visit the Menards Building Materials Desk or visit www.Menards.com.

19

Plan #M07-058D-0078

Lovely, Spacious Floor Plan

1,558 total square feet of living area

3 bedrooms, 2 baths

2-car garage

Basement foundation

Special features

Energy efficient home with 2" x 6" exterior walls

The spacious utility room is located conveniently between the garage and kitchen/dining area

The bedrooms are separated from the living area by a hallway

An enormous living area with fireplace and vaulted ceiling opens to the kitchen and dining area

The master bedroom is enhanced with a large bay window, walk-in closet and private bath

Price Code B

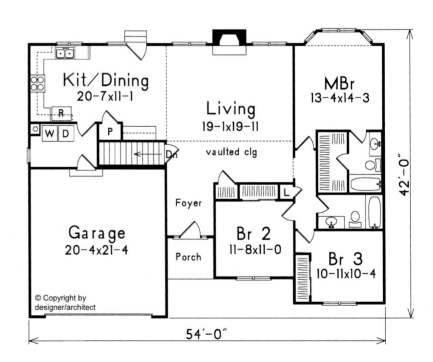

Kit/Dining
20-7x11-1

Living
19-1x19-11
vaulted clg

MBr
13-4x14-3

W D P

R

Dn

Foyer

L

Garage
20-4x21-4

Br 2
11-8x11-0

Br 3
10-11x10-4

Porch

© Copyright by designer/architect

42'-0"

54'-0"

Plan #M07-072L-0013

Pleasant Country Cottage

1,283 total square feet of living area

3 bedrooms, 2 baths

2-car garage

Basement foundation

Special features

The fabulous great room is just off the front foyer and boasts a dramatic vaulted ceiling and cozy fireplace

The efficient kitchen enjoys a pantry and sunny breakfast room with deck access

Bedroom #2 boasts a cozy window seat

Price Code D

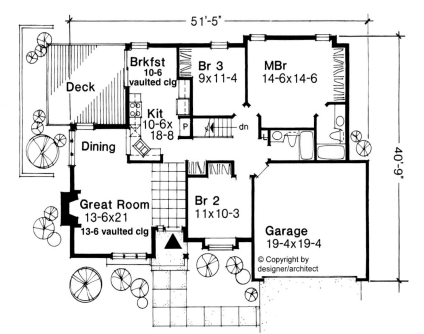

To order this plan, visit the Menards Building Materials Desk or visit www.Menards.com.

21

MENARDS

Plan #M07-033D-0002

Striking, Covered Arched Entry

1,859 total square feet of living area

3 bedrooms, 2 1/2 baths

2-car garage

Basement foundation

Special features

A fireplace highlights the vaulted great room

The master bedroom includes a large closet and private bath

The kitchen adjoins the breakfast room providing easy access to the outdoors

Price Code D

Br 2
10-8x11-3

MBr
11-10x17-2

Dn

open to below

Br 3
11-8x10-2

Second Floor
789 sq. ft.

63'-4"

36'-0"

Brk
9-8x
11-6

Kit
10-0x13-8

Great Rm
15-2x19-0

vaulted

Up

Dn

Foyer

Dining
11-8x11-2

Garage
21-8x21-8

© Copyright by designer/architect

First Floor
1,070 sq. ft.

Rear View

To order this plan, visit the Menards Building Materials Desk or visit www.Menards.com.

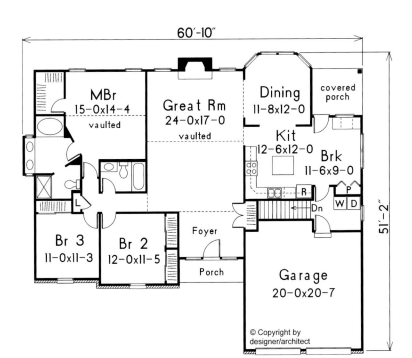

Plan #M07-001D-0013

Traditional Exterior, Handsome Accents

1,882 total square feet of living area

3 bedrooms, 2 baths

2-car garage

Basement foundation

Special features

A wide, handsome entrance opens to the vaulted great room with fireplace

The great room and dining area are conveniently joined but still allow privacy

A private covered porch extends the breakfast area

A practical passageway runs through the laundry room from the garage to the kitchen

There is a vaulted ceiling in the master bedroom

Price Code D

Floor plan dimensions and rooms:

60'-10"

51'-2"

- MBr 15-0x14-4 vaulted
- Great Rm 24-0x17-0 vaulted
- Dining 11-8x12-0
- covered porch
- Kit 12-6x12-0
- Brk 11-6x9-0
- Br 3 11-0x11-3
- Br 2 12-0x11-5
- Foyer
- Porch
- Garage 20-0x20-7
- Dn
- W D
- R
- P
- L

© Copyright by designer/architect

Rear View

To order this plan, visit the *Menards Building Materials Desk* or visit www.Menards.com.

23

Plan #M07-065L-0002

Exciting Roof Lines

2,101 total square feet of living area

3 bedrooms, 2 1/2 baths

2-car garage

Basement foundation

Special features

The sunken great room has a balcony above

The octagon-shaped master bedroom is spacious and private

Luxurious amenities are located throughout this modest sized home

Price Code C

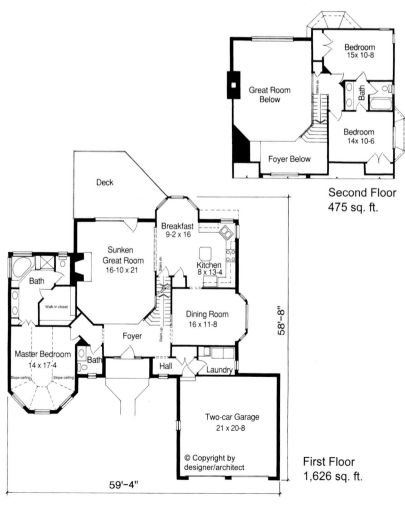

Second Floor
475 sq. ft.

First Floor
1,626 sq. ft.

To order this plan, visit the *Menards Building Materials Desk* or visit www.Menards.com.

Plan #M07-065L-0166

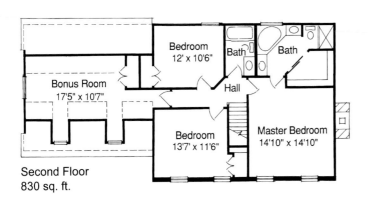

Second Floor
830 sq. ft.

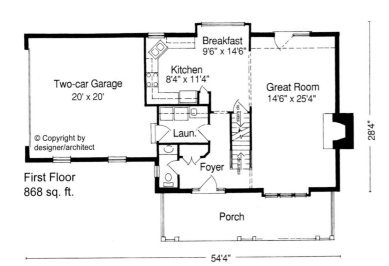

First Floor
868 sq. ft.

Efficient Two-Story Home

1,698 total square feet of living area

3 bedrooms, 2 1/2 baths

2-car side entry garage

Basement or crawl space foundation, please specify when ordering

Special features

The massive great room runs the entire depth of the home offering a view of the front porch and easy access to the backyard

The adjacent breakfast area offers a relaxed atmosphere and enjoys close proximity to the U-shaped kitchen

All bedrooms are located on the second floor, including the master bedroom that features a deluxe bath and walk-in closet

The optional bonus room over the garage has an additional 269 square feet of living area

Price Code B

To order this plan, visit the *Menards* Building Materials Desk or visit www.Menards.com.

Plan #M07-024L-0624

Inviting Front Porch

3,223 total square feet of living area

4 bedrooms, 4 baths

2-car drive under garage

Pier foundation

Special features

Outdoor living will be enjoyable in this home with an abundance of porch and deck space for entertaining

The large and open living room accesses the porch through three separate doors

The two bedrooms and exercise room on the second floor all have their own walk-in closets for extra storage space

Price Code F

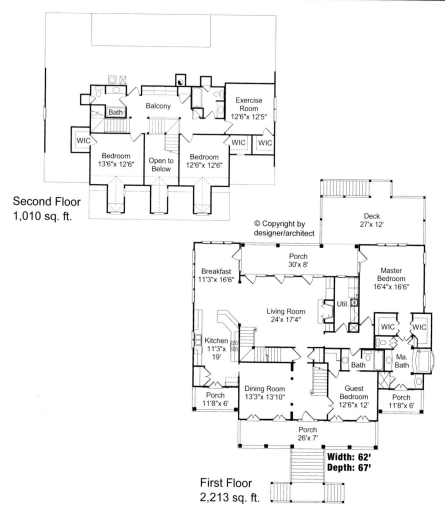

Second Floor
1,010 sq. ft.

© Copyright by designer/architect

First Floor
2,213 sq. ft.

Width: 62'
Depth: 67'

To order this plan, visit the *Menards Building Materials Desk* or visit *www.Menards.com.*

Plan #M07-072L-0024

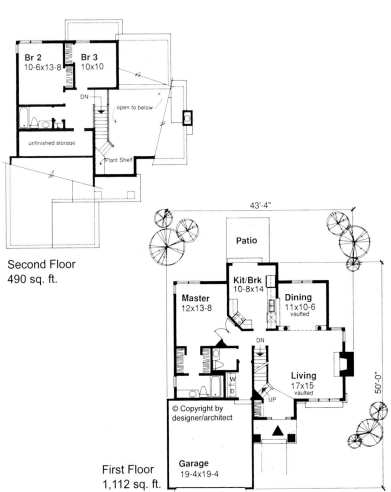

Second Floor
490 sq. ft.

First Floor
1,112 sq. ft.

Stunning Two-Story

1,602 total square feet of living area

3 bedrooms, 2 1/2 baths

2-car garage

Basement foundation

Special features

The vaulted living room shines with a two-story window and grand fireplace

Columns define the entry into the formal dining room

A double-door entry adds elegance to the master suite that also enjoys two closets and a private bath

Price Code D

To order this plan, visit the Menards Building Materials Desk or visit www.Menards.com.

27

Plan #M07-039L-0017

Covered Front Porch

1,966 total square feet of living area

3 bedrooms, 2 1/2 baths

2-car side entry garage

Basement foundation

Special features

A private dining room remains the focal point when entering the home

The kitchen and breakfast area join to create a functional area

Lots of closet space can be found in all the second floor bedrooms

Price Code C

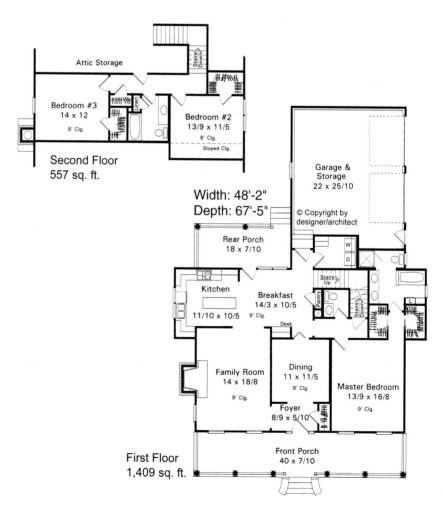

Attic Storage

Stairs Down

Bedroom #3
14 x 12
8' Clg.

Linen

Bedroom #2
13/9 x 11/5
8' Clg.
Sloped Clg.

Second Floor
557 sq. ft.

Garage & Storage
22 x 25/10

Width: 48'-2"
Depth: 67'-5"

© Copyright by designer/architect

Rear Porch
18 x 7/10

W
D

Stairs Up

Kitchen
11/10 x 10/5

Breakfast
14/3 x 10/5
9' Clg.

Pantry

Stairs Down

Desk

Family Room
14 x 18/8
9' Clg.

Dining
11 x 11/5
9' Clg.

Master Bedroom
13/9 x 16/8
9' Clg.

Foyer
8/9 x 5/10

First Floor
1,409 sq. ft.

Front Porch
40 x 7/10

To order this plan, visit the *Menards* Building Materials Desk or visit www.Menards.com.

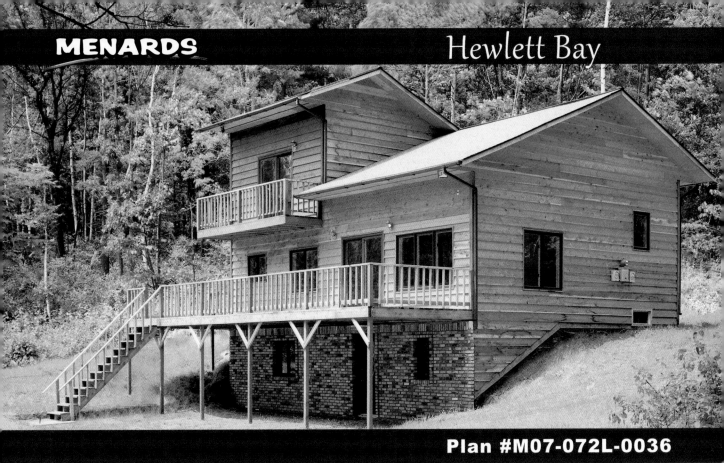

Plan #M07-072L-0036

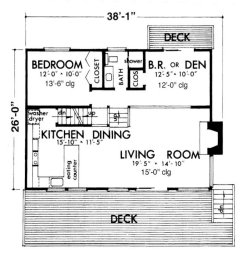

First Floor
936 sq. ft.

Second Floor
252 sq. ft.

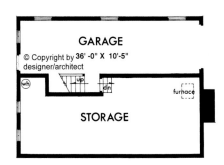

Lower Level

Wonderful Outdoor Living Spaces

1,188 total square feet of living area

3 bedrooms, 2 baths

1-car drive under side entry garage

Walk-out basement foundation

Special features

The large living room with fireplace enjoys a ceiling height of 15' and access to the large deck

The second floor bedroom is a nice escape with its own bath and private deck

A large eating counter in the kitchen creates casual dining space

Price Code D

To order this plan, visit the Menards Building Materials Desk or visit www.Menards.com.

29

Plan #M07-007D-0127

Luxury Home For Narrow Site Has Exciting Interior

2,158 total square feet of living area

3 bedrooms, 2 1/2 baths

2-car garage

Basement foundation

Special features

The vaulted entry has a coat closet and built-in shelves with a plant shelf above

The two-story living room has tall dramatic windows flanking the fireplace

A laundry and half bath are located near the kitchen that has over 30' of counterspace

The vaulted master bedroom has a window seat and two walk-in closets

Price Code C

Rear View

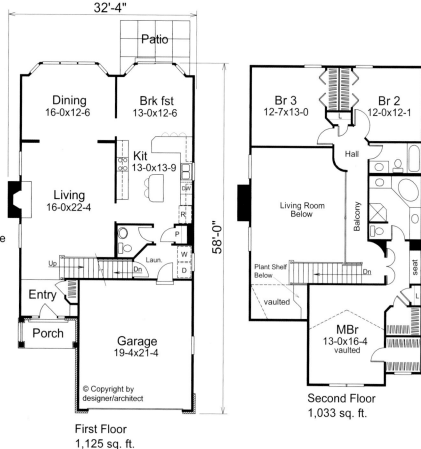

First Floor
1,125 sq. ft.

Second Floor
1,033 sq. ft.

32'-4"

58'-0"

Patio

Dining 16-0x12-6

Brk fst 13-0x12-6

Kit 13-0x13-9

Living 16-0x22-4

Laun.

Up

Dn

Entry

Porch

Garage 19-4x21-4

© Copyright by designer/architect

Br 3 12-7x13-0

Br 2 12-0x12-1

Hall

Living Room Below

Balcony

Plant Shelf Below

Dn

vaulted

seat

MBr 13-0x16-4 vaulted

To order this plan, visit the *Menards* Building Materials Desk or visit www.Menards.com.

Plan #M07-121D-0002

Double Dormers And Gables Add Curb Appeal

2,025 total square feet of living area

3 bedrooms, 2 1/2 baths

2-car side entry garage

Basement foundation

Special features

The cozy great room enjoys a 42" wood burning fireplace as the main focal point

The dining room has decorative columns and beams along with a vaulted ceiling

The vaulted kitchen has a versatile cooktop island with separate oven

An elegant coffered ceiling tops the private master bedroom

2" x 6" exterior walls available, please order plan #M07-121E-0002

Price Code B

69'-8"

42'-8"

Patio

MBr
15-4x15-1
Coffer Clg

Great Rm
22-4x15-0
Vaulted

Kitchen
10-9x16-4
Vaulted

Pow Rm

Brkfst
11-5x16-4
Vaulted

Laun/
Mud Rm

Desk

Plant Shelf

Dining Rm
14-0x12-10
Vaulted

Entry

Garage
23-4x23-0

Br 2
11-4x10-4
Vaulted

Br 3
11-8x10-4
Vaulted

Porch

© Copyright by designer/architect

Vaulted

Rear View

To order this plan, visit the Menards Building Materials Desk or visit www.Menards.com.

31

Plan #M07-058D-0072

Year-Round Or Weekend Getaway Home

1,339 total square feet of living area

3 bedrooms, 2 1/2 baths

Crawl space foundation

Special features

Energy efficient home with 2" x 6" exterior walls

A full-length covered porch enhances the front facade

The vaulted ceiling and stone fireplace add drama to the family room

Walk-in closets in the bedrooms provide ample storage space

A combined kitchen/dining area adjoins the family room for the perfect entertaining space

Price Code A

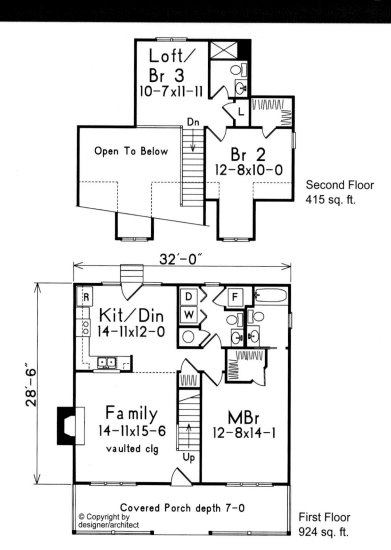

Loft/ Br 3
10-7x11-11

Open To Below

Dn

Br 2
12-8x10-0

Second Floor
415 sq. ft.

32'-0"

28'-6"

Kit/Din
14-11x12-0

R   D   F
W

Family
14-11x15-6
vaulted clg

Up

MBr
12-8x14-1

Covered Porch depth 7-0

© Copyright by designer/architect

First Floor
924 sq. ft.

To order this plan, visit the Menards Building Materials Desk or visit www.Menards.com.

Plan #M07-024L-0042

Grand Two-Story Living Room

1,880 total square feet of living area

3 bedrooms, 2 1/2 baths

Crawl space foundation

Special features

The large front porch is a perfect spot to sit back and relax

The first floor bedroom includes a private bath with a double-bowl vanity and a walk-in closet, making it an ideal master suite

The secondary bedrooms enjoy walk-in closets and share a Jack and Jill bath

Price Code C

Open to Below

Bedroom 12'6"x 11"

Balcony

Bedroom 10'6"x 10'9"

Second Floor 636 sq. ft.

© Copyright by designer/architect

Width: 40'-6"
Depth: 40'-0"

Deck

Living 14'6"x 17'6"

Breakfast 9'8"x 10'6"

Bedroom 12'6"x 15'

WIC

Kitch. 9'8"x 11'1"

Dining 10'8"x 12'

Foyer

Porch

First Floor 1,244 sq. ft.

To order this plan, visit the Menards Building Materials Desk or visit www.Menards.com.

33

Marlow Manor

Plan #M07-055L-0043

Built-In Pantry

1,654 total square feet of living area

3 bedrooms, 2 baths

2-car garage

Walk-out basement, basement, crawl space or slab foundation, please specify when ordering

Special features

The U-shaped kitchen features lots of cabinetry, counter seating and access to the dining room/hearth room

The great room has a sloped ceiling, media center and fireplace

The master bath is accented with glass blocks above the whirlpool tub

Price Code C

Plan #M07-029D-0002

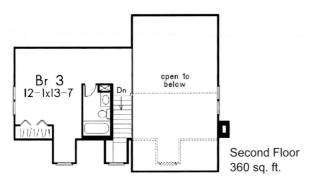

Br 3
12-1x13-7

open to below

Dn

Second Floor
360 sq. ft.

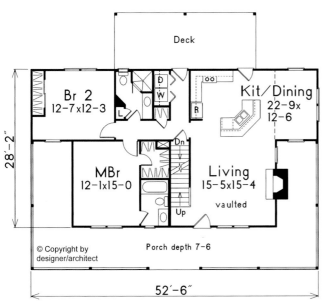

Deck

Br 2
12-7x12-3

D

W

L

Kit/Dining
22-9x
12-6

R

28'-2"

MBr
12-1x15-0

Dn

Living
15-5x15-4

Up

vaulted

© Copyright by
designer/architect

Porch depth 7-6

52'-6"

First Floor
1,259 sq. ft.

Country-Style
Porch Adds Charm

1,619 total square feet of living area

3 bedrooms, 3 baths

Basement foundation, drawings also
include crawl space and slab foundations

Special features

The second floor has a private bedroom
and bath

The kitchen features a snack bar and
adjacent dining area

The master bedroom has a private bath
and walk-in closet

The washer and dryer closet is centrally
located for convenience

Price Code B

Rear View

To order this plan, visit the Menards Building Materials Desk or visit www.Menards.com.

35

Eureka

Plan #M07-122D-0001

Energy Efficient
Two-Story Berm Home

1,105 total square feet of living area

2 bedrooms, 1 1/2 baths

Slab foundation

Special features

Energy efficient home with 2" x 6" exterior walls

This fresh, modern design enjoys sleek window lines and a stucco exterior making it a truly one-of-a-kind living experience

The compact, yet efficient U-shaped kitchen offers a tremendous amount of counterspace within reach for all sorts of kitchen tasks at hand

A tall sloped ceiling in the two-story living room gives this home an open and spacious feel all those who enter will appreciate

Price Code AAA

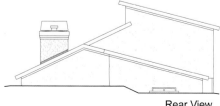

Rear View

33'-0"

© Copyright by designer/architect

Bedroom 2
11-9x11-4

Dining
9-4x7-8

Kitchen
9-0x9-0

Hall

Bath

Lndry

Living Rm
17-8x14-11

Sloped Clg.

Foyer

35'-0"

Patio

First Floor
880 sq. ft.

Bath

Bedroom 1
11-10x14-2

Open

Second Floor
225 sq. ft.

To order this plan, visit the Menards Building Materials Desk or visit www.Menards.com.

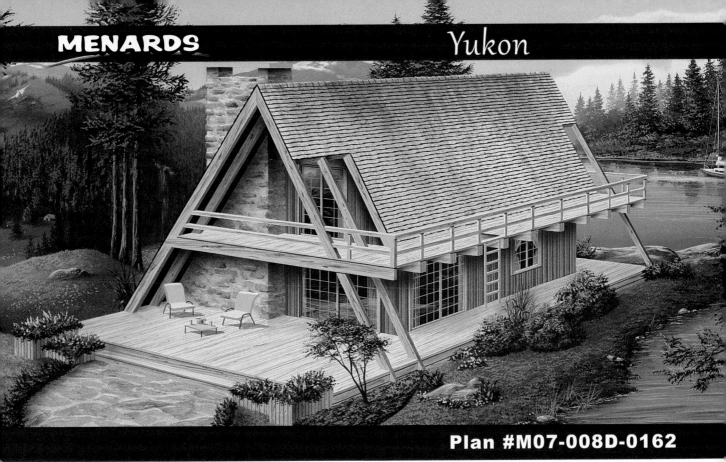

Plan #M07-008D-0162

Terrific Design
Loaded With Extras

865 total square feet of living area

2 bedrooms, 1 bath

Pier foundation

Special features

The central living area provides an enormous amount of space for gathering around the fireplace

The outdoor ladder on the wrap-around deck connects the top deck with the main deck

The kitchen is bright and cheerful with lots of windows and access to the deck

Price Code AAA

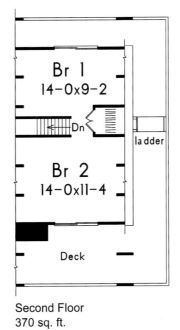

21'-0"

Stor

Deck

Kit
10-4x
9-2

R

Up

ladder

24'-0"

Living
20-4x11-8

© Copyright by
designer/architect

Deck

First Floor
495 sq. ft.

Br 1
14-0x9-2

Dn

ladder

Br 2
14-0x11-4

Deck

Second Floor
370 sq. ft.

To order this plan, visit the *Menards* Building Materials Desk or visit www.Menards.com.

37

Plan #M07-007D-0198

Simple, Affordable Lake Home

1,142 total square feet of living area

2 bedrooms, 1 1/2 baths

1-car side entry garage

Walk-out basement foundation

Special features

The living room has a bayed dining area with sliding glass doors to a large rear deck

The U-shaped kitchen has a separate laundry space and pass-through eating bar

The lower level consists of a hall bath, linen closet and two bedrooms with walk-in closets and sliding glass doors to the patio

Price Code AA

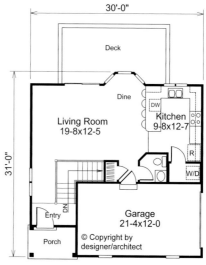

First Floor
572 sq. ft.

30'-0"

31'-0"

Deck

Dine

Living Room
19-8x12-5

Kitchen
9-8x12-7

DW

R

W/D

Garage
21-4x12-0

Entry

DN

Porch

© Copyright by designer/architect

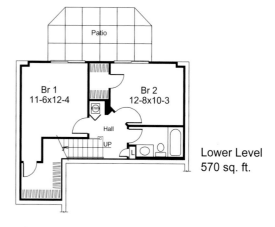

Lower Level
570 sq. ft.

Patio

Br 1
11-6x12-4

Br 2
12-8x10-3

Hall

UP

Rear View

To order this plan, visit the Menards Building Materials Desk or visit www.Menards.com.

Plan #M07-022D-0001

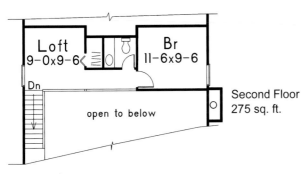

Loft
9-0x9-6

Br
11-6x9-6

Dn

open to below

Second Floor
275 sq. ft.

30'-0"

Porch

Kit
9-6x
12-0

D
W

Br
11-6x11-6

R

Stor.

Up

Stor.

33'-5"

Living/Dining
26-0x11-6

© Copyright by
designer/architect

Deck

First Floor
764 sq. ft.

A Vacation Home For All Seasons

1,039 total square feet of living area

2 bedrooms, 1 1/2 baths

Crawl space foundation

Special features

Cathedral construction provides the maximum in living area openness

Expansive glass viewing walls create an open feeling in the living/dining area

Two decks, front and back

This home has a charming second story loft arrangement

Simple, low-maintenance construction

Price Code AA

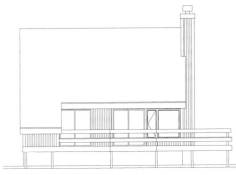

Rear View

To order this plan, visit the *Menards* Building Materials Desk or visit www.Menards.com.

39

Morfontaine

MENARDS

Plan #M07-077L-0026

Vaulted Great Room

1,501 total square feet of living area

3 bedrooms, 2 baths

2-car garage

Slab, basement or crawl space foundation, please specify when ordering

Special features

The friendly covered porch with arched openings invites guests inside and adds stunning curb appeal

The exquisite great room offers a vaulted ceiling and grand fireplace flanked by built-in cabinets

The beautiful master bedroom features a trayed ceiling, two walk-in closets and a plush bath with garden tub

Price Code D

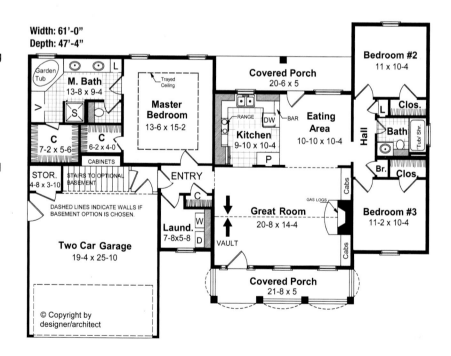

Width: 61'-0"
Depth: 47'-4"

Garden Tub

L

M. Bath 13-8 x 9-4

Trayed Ceiling

Master Bedroom 13-6 x 15-2

Covered Porch 20-6 x 5

Bedroom #2 11 x 10-4

C 7-2 x 5-6

C 6-2 x 4-0

RANGE

DW

BAR

Eating Area 10-10 x 10-4

L

Clos.

Kitchen 9-10 x 10-4

P

Hall

Bath

Tub/Shr.

CABINETS

STOR. 4-8 x 3-10

STAIRS TO OPTIONAL BASEMENT

ENTRY

Br.

Clos.

DASHED LINES INDICATE WALLS IF BASEMENT OPTION IS CHOSEN.

C

GAS LOGS

Cabs

Great Room 20-8 x 14-4

Bedroom #3 11-2 x 10-4

Laund. 7-8x5-8

W

D

Two Car Garage 19-4 x 25-10

VAULT

Cabs

© Copyright by designer/architect

Covered Porch 21-8 x 5

To order this plan, visit the Menards Building Materials Desk or visit www.Menards.com.

Plan #M07-001D-0102

Country-Style With Spacious Rooms

1,197 total square feet of living area

3 bedrooms, 1 bath

Crawl space foundation, drawings also include basement and slab foundations

Special features

Energy efficient home with 2" x 6" exterior walls

The U-shaped kitchen includes ample workspace, a breakfast bar, laundry area and direct access to the outdoors

A large living room has a convenient coat closet

The master bedroom features a large walk-in closet

Price Code AA

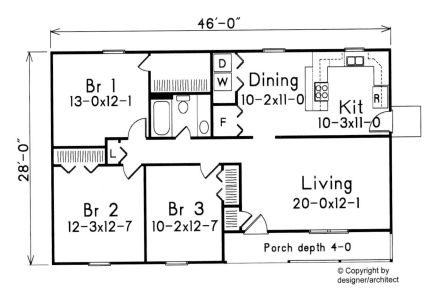

46'-0"

28'-0"

Br 1
13-0x12-1

D
W
F

Dining
10-2x11-0

Kit
10-3x11-0

R

L

Br 2
12-3x12-7

Br 3
10-2x12-7

Living
20-0x12-1

Porch depth 4-0

© Copyright by designer/architect

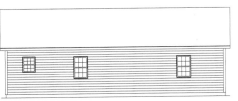

Rear View

To order this plan, visit the *Menards* Building Materials Desk or visit www.Menards.com.

41

Plan #M07-024L-0002

Central Living Room Is Great For Gathering

1,405 total square feet of living area

3 bedrooms, 2 baths

Slab foundation

Special features

The compact design has all the luxuries of a larger home

The master bedroom has its privacy away from other bedrooms

The living room has a corner fireplace, access to the outdoors and easily reaches the dining area and kitchen

A large utility room near the kitchen has access to the outdoors

Price Code A

Width: 42'
Depth: 51'

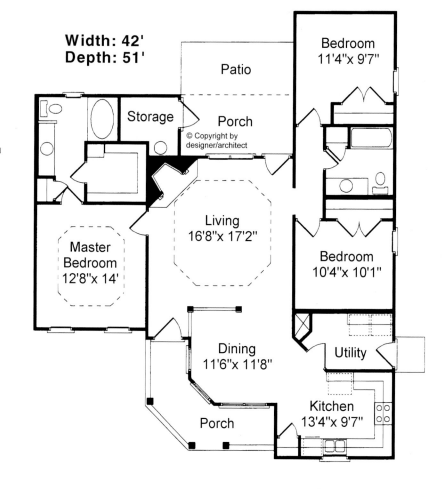

Patio

Storage

Porch

© Copyright by designer/architect

Bedroom
11'4"x 9'7"

Living
16'8"x 17'2"

Master
Bedroom
12'8"x 14'

Bedroom
10'4"x 10'1"

Dining
11'6"x 11'8"

Utility

Porch

Kitchen
13'4"x 9'7"

Plan #M07-008D-0069

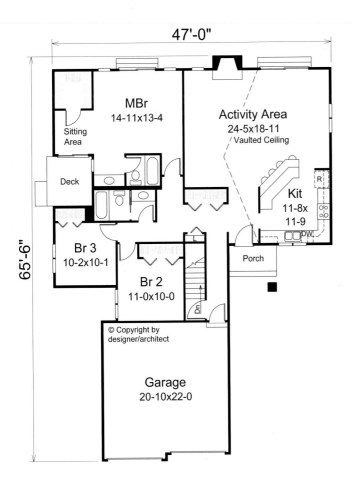

47'-0"

65'-6"

MBr
14-11x13-4

Sitting Area

Deck

Activity Area
24-5x18-11
/ Vaulted Ceiling

Kit
11-8x
11-9

R

DW

Br 3
10-2x10-1

Br 2
11-0x10-0

Porch

Dn

© Copyright by designer/architect

Garage
20-10x22-0

Multiple Gabled Roofs Add Drama

1,533 total square feet of living area

3 bedrooms, 2 baths

2-car garage

Partial basement foundation, drawings also include crawl space foundation

Special features

The master bedroom accesses the outdoors through sliding glass doors onto a deck

A sloped ceiling adds volume to the large activity area

The activity area has a fireplace, a snack bar and shares access to the outdoors with the master bedroom

A convenient utility room is located near the garage

Price Code B

Zoey

Plan #M07-121D-0023

Handsome Ranch Home With Shingle Siding

1,762 total square feet of living area

3 bedrooms, 2 baths

2-car garage

Basement foundation

Special features

The vaulted great room boasts a warming corner fireplace and flows into the vaulted dining area

An island with eating bar in the kitchen is a perfect gathering spot for casual meals

A private bath, large walk-in closet and vaulted ceiling are some of the amenities of the master bedroom

Price Code A

Rear View

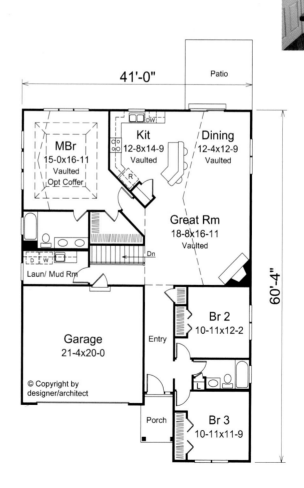

Patio

41'-0"

MBr
15-0x16-11
Vaulted
Opt Coffer

Kit
12-8x14-9
Vaulted

Dining
12-4x12-9
Vaulted

Great Rm
18-8x16-11
Vaulted

Dn

Laun/ Mud Rm

Garage
21-4x20-0

© Copyright by
designer/architect

Entry

Br 2
10-11x12-2

60'-4"

Porch

Br 3
10-11x11-9

44

Plan #M07-037D-0009

Country Charm
Wrapped In A Veranda

2,059 total square feet of living area

3 bedrooms, 2 1/2 baths

2-car detached garage

Slab foundation, drawings also include basement and crawl space foundations

Special features

9' ceilings throughout the home

The octagon-shaped breakfast room has plenty of windows and offers a view to the veranda

The first floor master bedroom has a large walk-in closet and deluxe bath

The secondary bedrooms and bath feature dormers and are adjacent to the cozy sitting area

Price Code C

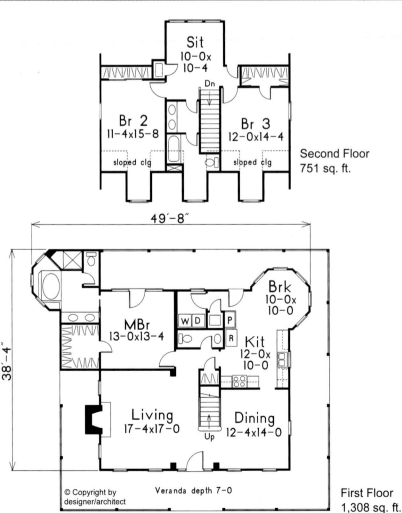

Sit 10-0x 10-4

Dn

Br 2 11-4x15-8

Br 3 12-0x14-4

sloped clg   sloped clg

Second Floor 751 sq. ft.

49'-8"

38'-4"

MBr 13-0x13-4

Brk 10-0x 10-0

W D   P
R

Kit 12-0x 10-0

Living 17-4x17-0

Up

Dining 12-4x14-0

© Copyright by designer/architect

Veranda depth 7-0

First Floor 1,308 sq. ft.

Rear View

Plan #M07-024L-0043

Home Is Flooded With Natural Light

1,768 total square feet of living area

3 bedrooms, 2 1/2 baths

Slab or crawl space foundation, please specify when ordering

Special features

Upon entering you will get a feeling of spaciousness with the two-story living and dining rooms

The bayed breakfast area is a refreshing place to start the day

The covered porch off the breakfast area extends dining to the outdoors

Price Code C

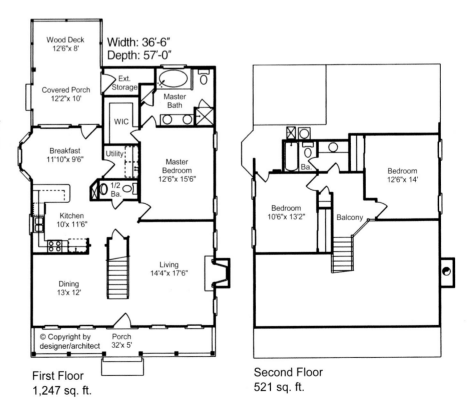

Width: 36'-6"
Depth: 57'-0"

Wood Deck 12'6"x 8'

Covered Porch 12'2"x 10'

Ext. Storage

Master Bath

WIC

Breakfast 11'10"x 9'6"

Utility

Master Bedroom 12'6"x 15'6"

1/2 Ba.

Kitchen 10'x 11'6"

Dining 13'x 12'

Living 14'4"x 17'6"

© Copyright by designer/architect

Porch 32'x 5'

First Floor
1,247 sq. ft.

Ba.

Bedroom 12'6"x 14'

Bedroom 10'6"x 13'2"

Balcony

Second Floor
521 sq. ft.

Plan #M07-017D-0010

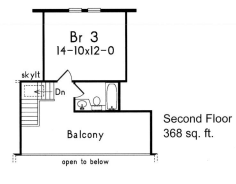

Br 3
14-10x12-0

skylt

Dn

Balcony

open to below

Second Floor
368 sq. ft.

41'-5"

44'-1"

Br 2
11-0x12-0

MBr
12-0x12-0

Equip.

Up

W D

L

R

Kitchen
12-7x7-6

Living
12-9x15-7
vaulted

Dining
12-9x14-0
vaulted

Deck

© Copyright by
designer/architect

First Floor
1,292 sq. ft.

Dramatic Expanse Of Windows

1,660 total square feet of living area

3 bedrooms, 3 baths

Partial basement/crawl space foundation, drawings also include slab foundation

Special features

Energy efficient home with 2" x 6" exterior walls

The convenient equipment room has closet space for extra storage

Spacious living and dining rooms look even larger with the openness of the foyer and kitchen

A large wrap-around deck is a great plus for outdoor living

A broad balcony overlooks the living and dining rooms

Price Code C

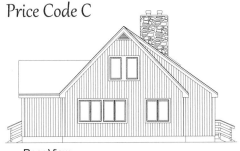

Rear View

Jillian

Plan #M07-121D-0005

Cozy Corner Fireplace
In Great Room

1,562 total square feet of living area

3 bedrooms, 2 baths

2-car garage

Basement foundation

Special features

The formal dining room is graced with an open feeling thanks to the beautiful vaulted ceiling and decorative corner columns

A wrap-around breakfast bar has enough seating for five people and overlooks the large and spacious great room

All the bedrooms are located near each other for convenient family living

Price Code A

Rear View

Floor plan dimensions: 65'-0" wide, 46'-4" deep

- MBr 14-3x13-3, Coffer Clg
- Br 2 11-0x10-2
- Br 3 10-6x10-2
- Great Rm 15-9x16-0, Vaulted
- Brkfst 10-8x11-7, Vaulted
- Kitchen 10-8x11-9, Vaulted
- Dining 10-1x11-4, Vaulted
- Foyer
- Porch, Vaulted
- Plant Shelf
- Laun/Mud Rm
- Garage 20-8x21-4
- Patio

© Copyright by designer/architect

To order this plan, visit the *Menards* Building Materials Desk or visit *www.Menards.com.*

Plan #M07-024L-0008

Ideal Vacation Style For Views

1,650 total square feet of living area

4 bedrooms, 2 baths

Pier or crawl space foundation, please specify when ordering

Special features

The master bedroom is located on the second floor for privacy

The open living area connects to the dining area

The two-story living area features lots of windows for views to the outdoors and a large fireplace

The kitchen boasts a center island and access to the rear porch

Price Code B

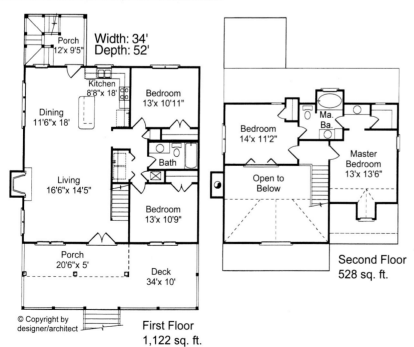

Width: 34'
Depth: 52'

Porch
12'x 9'5"

Kitchen
8'8"x 18'

Dining
11'6"x 18'

Bedroom
13'x 10'11"

Bath

Living
16'6"x 14'5"

Bedroom
13'x 10'9"

Porch
20'6"x 5'

Deck
34'x 10'

© Copyright by
designer/architect

First Floor
1,122 sq. ft.

Bedroom
14'x 11'2"

Ma. Ba.

Open to Below

Master Bedroom
13'x 13'6"

Second Floor
528 sq. ft.

To order this plan, visit the Menards Building Materials Desk or visit www.Menards.com.

49

Wellington

Plan #M07-003D-0001

Practical Two-Story, Full Of Features

2,058 total square feet of living area

3 bedrooms, 2 1/2 baths

2-car garage

Basement foundation, drawings also include slab and crawl space foundations

Special features

A handsome two-story foyer with balcony creates a spacious entrance area

The vaulted master bedroom has a private dressing area and large walk-in closet

Skylights furnish the full baths with natural light

The laundry closet is conveniently located on the second floor near the bedrooms

Price Code C

Rear View

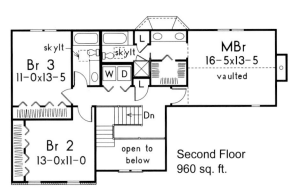

Second Floor 960 sq. ft.

- Br 3 11-0x13-5
- MBr 16-5x13-5 vaulted
- Br 2 13-0x11-0
- open to below
- skylt
- W D
- L
- L
- Dn

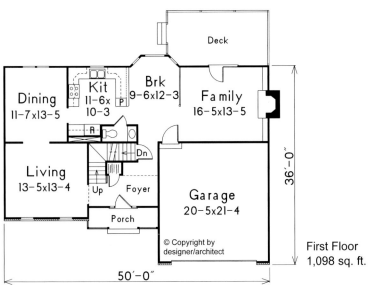

First Floor 1,098 sq. ft.

- Deck
- Dining 11-7x13-5
- Kit 11-6x 10-3
- Brk 9-6x12-3
- Family 16-5x13-5
- Living 13-5x13-4
- Foyer
- Up
- Dn
- Garage 20-5x21-4
- Porch
- © Copyright by designer/architect
- 50'-0"
- 36'-0"

To order this plan, visit the Menards Building Materials Desk or visit www.Menards.com.

Plan #M07-001D-0081

Large Great Room And Dining Area

1,160 total square feet of living area

3 bedrooms, 1 1/2 baths

Crawl space foundation, drawings also include basement and slab foundations

Special features

The U-shaped kitchen includes a breakfast bar and convenient laundry closet

The master bedroom features a private half bath and large closet

The dining area has outdoor access

The dining area and great rooms combine to create an open living atmosphere

Price Code AA

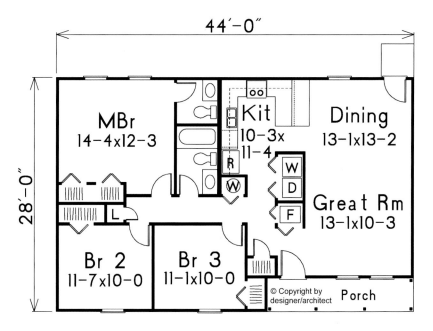

Rear View

To order this plan, visit the Menards Building Materials Desk or visit www.Menards.com.

51

San Saguaro

Plan #M07-007D-0222

Two Patio Home With Courtyard

1,522 total square feet of living area

3 bedrooms, 2 baths

2-car garage

Crawl space foundation, drawings also include slab foundation

Special features

This open floor plan design has 9' ceilings and is perfect for a narrow lot

A cozy covered porch leads to an entry that's open to a large U-shaped kitchen with snack bar, built-in pantry, abundant cabinets and 26 linear feet of counter space

A walk-in closet, double-entry doors and luxury bath are features of the master bedroom

Price Code A

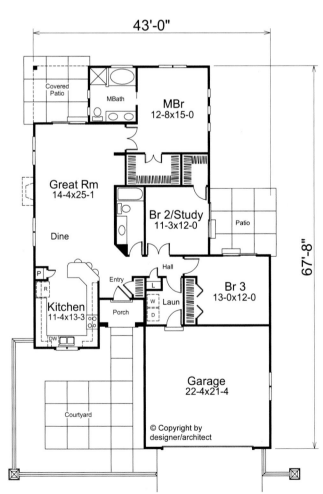

Rear View

To order this plan, visit the Menards Building Materials Desk or visit www.Menards.com.

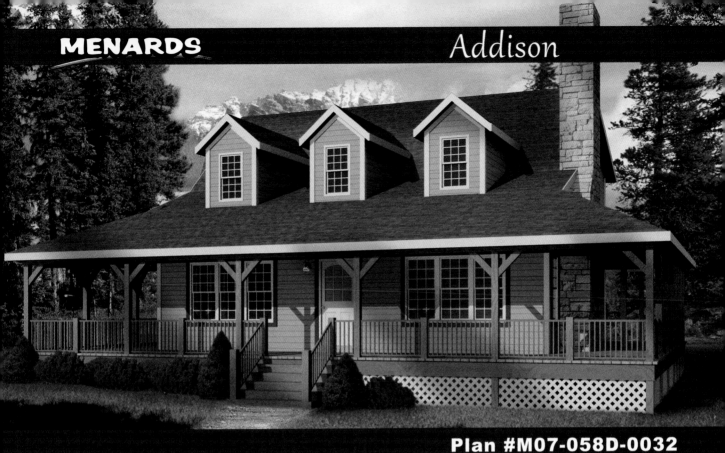

Plan #M07-058D-0032

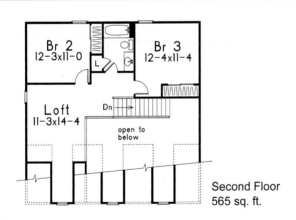

Br 2
12-3x11-0

Br 3
12-4x11-4

L

Loft
11-3x14-4

Dn

open to
below

Second Floor
565 sq. ft.

Charming Wrap-Around Porch

1,879 total square feet of living area

3 bedrooms, 2 baths

Crawl space foundation

Special features

An open floor plan on both floors makes
this home appear larger

The loft area overlooks the great room or can
become an optional fourth bedroom

A large storage area in the rear of home has
access from the exterior

Price Code C

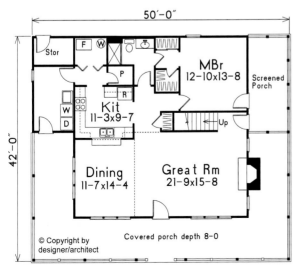

50'-0"

42'-0"

Stor

F W

MBr
12-10x13-8

Screened
Porch

P

R

Kit
11-3x9-7

Up

W
D

Dining
11-7x14-4

Great Rm
21-9x15-8

© Copyright by
designer/architect

Covered porch depth 8-0

First Floor
1,314 sq. ft.

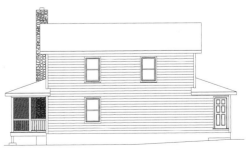

Rear View

Milner

MENARDS

Plan #M07-013L-0050

Beautiful Country Porch

2,098 total square feet of living area

3 bedrooms, 2 1/2 baths

3-car side entry detached garage

Crawl space or basement foundation, please specify when ordering

Special features

The covered porch wraps around the entire house, leading to the deck and screened porch in the back

The spacious country kitchen has plenty of cabinet space as well as counterspace

The convenient laundry chute is located near the second floor bathroom

Price Code D

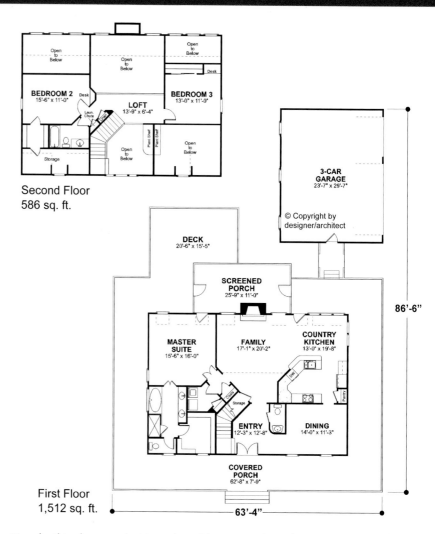

Second Floor
586 sq. ft.

First Floor
1,512 sq. ft.

54

Plan #M07-065L-0062

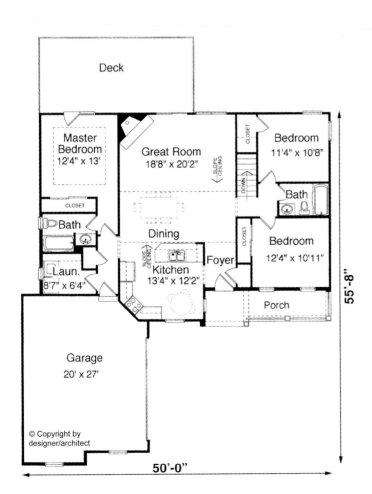

Deck

Master Bedroom
12'4" x 13'

Great Room
18'8" x 20'2"
SLOPE CEILING

CLOSET

DOWN

Bedroom
11'4" x 10'8"

CLOSET

Bath

CLOSET

Bath

Dining

SLOPE CEILING

Foyer

Kitchen
13'4" x 12'2"

Bedroom
12'4" x 10'11"

Laun.
8'7" x 6'4"

Porch

Garage
20' x 27'

© Copyright by designer/architect

50'-0"

55'-8"

Stone And Siding Create Charming Exterior

1,390 total square feet of living area

3 bedrooms, 2 baths

2-car side entry garage

Walk-out basement foundation

Special features

The kitchen with snack bar opens to the spacious great room with plenty of space for dining

A corner fireplace warms the adjoining great room and kitchen

The master bedroom is a relaxing retreat with a private bath and deck access

The secondary bedrooms are separated from the master bedroom and share a full bath

Price Code A

To order this plan, visit the Menards Building Materials Desk or visit www.Menards.com.

55

Plan #M07-010D-0001

Circle-Top Windows Adorn The Foyer

1,516 total square feet of living area

3 bedrooms, 2 1/2 baths

2-car garage

Basement foundation

Special features

The stairway to the second floor looks out over the living room

The master bedroom enjoys first floor privacy and a luxurious bath

The kitchen has easy access to the deck, laundry closet and garage

Price Code B

Rear View

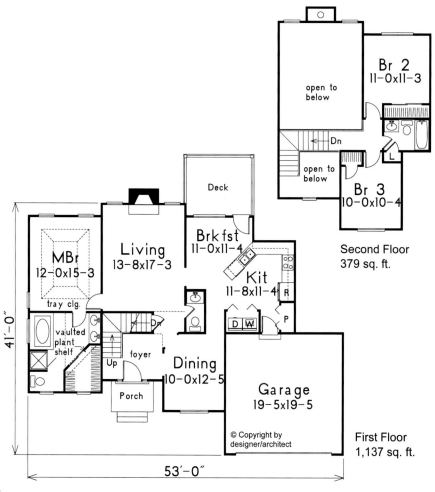

To order this plan, visit the *Menards Building Materials Desk* or visit www.Menards.com.

Plan #M07-007D-0061

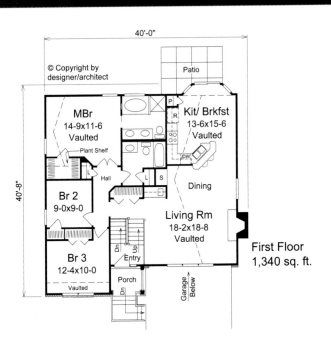

40'-0"

© Copyright by designer/architect

Patio

MBr
14-9x11-6
Vaulted

Plant Shelf

Kit/ Brkfst
13-6x15-6
Vaulted

Hall

Br 2
9-0x9-0

Dining

Br 3
12-4x10-0
Vaulted

Living Rm
18-2x18-8
Vaulted

Entry

Porch

Garage Below

40'-8"

First Floor 1,340 sq. ft.

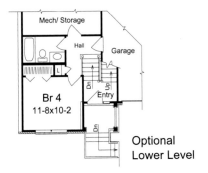

Mech/ Storage

Hall

Garage

Br 4
11-8x10-2

Entry

Optional Lower Level

Distinctive Home For Sloping Terrain

1,340 total square feet of living area

3 bedrooms, 2 baths

2-car drive under garage

Basement foundation

Special features

The vaulted living and dining rooms offer a fireplace, wet bar and breakfast counter

The vaulted master bedroom features a double-door entry, walk-in closet and bath

The basement includes a huge two-car garage and space for a bedroom/bath expansion

Optional lower level has an additional 636 square feet of living area

Price Code A

Rear View

To order this plan, visit the *Menards* Building Materials Desk or visit www.Menards.com.

57

Plan #M07-121D-0010

Vaulted Living Areas
For Added Spaciousness

1,281 total square feet of living area

3 bedrooms, 2 baths

2-car garage

Basement foundation

Special features

The functional vaulted kitchen features an angled raised counter perfect for a casual dining option

The vaulted great room and dining area combine, maximizing the interior for an open, airy feel

The vaulted master bedroom enjoys a walk-in closet and its own private bath

Price Code AA

Rear View

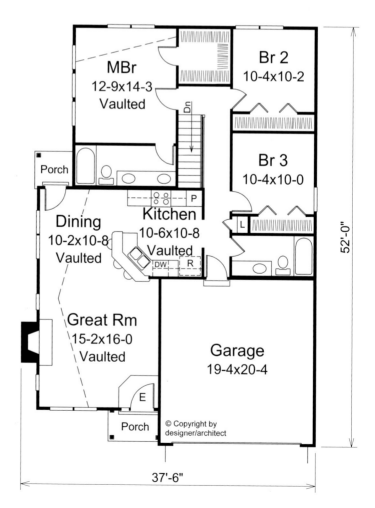

Plan #M07-014D-0005

Economical Ranch
For Easy Living

1,314 total square feet of living area

3 bedrooms, 2 baths

2-car garage

Basement foundation

Special features

Energy efficient home with 2" x 6" exterior walls

The covered porch adds immediate appeal and welcoming charm

The open floor plan combined with a vaulted ceiling offers spacious living

The functional kitchen is complete with a pantry and eating bar

The private master bedroom features a large walk-in closet and bath

Price Code A

Floor plan labels:

47'-0"

54'-0"

Patio

Br 2
10-0x 9-10

Br 3
10-0x 9-10

Kit
10-0x 9-10

Dining
11-0x11-0
vaulted

Dn

Living
15-6x15-0
vaulted

MBr
10-0x14-2

Porch depth 6-0

Garage
20-4x21-8

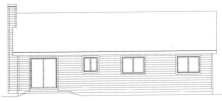

Rear View

To order this plan, visit the Menards Building Materials Desk or visit www.Menards.com.

59

Cumberland

Plan #M07-001D-0044

Distinctive Design, Convenient Floor Plan

1,375 total square feet of living area

3 bedrooms, 2 baths

2-car side entry garage

Crawl space foundation, drawings also include basement and slab foundations

Special features

Attractive gables highlight the home's exterior

The master bedroom features patio access, double walk-in closets and a private bath

The side entry garage includes a handy storage area

2" x 6" exterior walls available, please order plan #M07-001D-0101

Price Code A

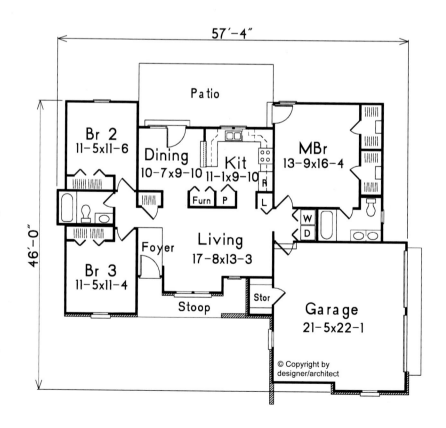

Rear View

To order this plan, visit the *Menards* Building Materials Desk or visit www.*Menards*.com.

Plan #M07-007D-0123

Second Floor
638 sq. ft.

Affordable Two-Story Has It All

1,308 total square feet of living area

3 bedrooms, 1 full bath, 2 half baths

2-car garage

Basement foundation

Special features

The multi-gabled facade and elongated porch create a pleasing country appeal

The large dining room with bay window and view to the rear patio opens to a full-functional kitchen with snack bar

An attractive U-shaped staircase with hall overlook leads to the second floor

Price Code A

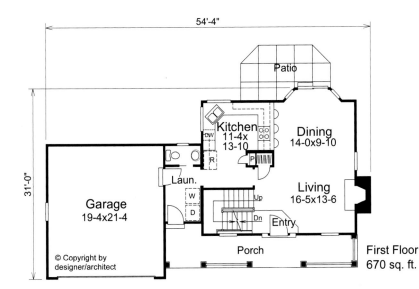

First Floor
670 sq. ft.

© Copyright by designer/architect

To order this plan, visit the Menards Building Materials Desk or visit www.Menards.com.

61

Plan #M07-040D-0026

Cozy Front Porch Welcomes Guests

1,393 total square feet of living area

3 bedrooms, 2 baths

2-car detached garage

Crawl space foundation, drawings also include slab foundation

Special features

The L-shaped kitchen features a walk-in pantry, island cooktop and is convenient to the laundry room and dining area

The master bedroom features a large walk-in closet and private bath with separate tub and shower

A lovely view of the patio can be seen from the dining area

Price Code B

Garage
21-4x23-4

© Copyright by designer/architect

Patio

Dining
13-4x9-8

Kitchen
13-4x10-0

MBr
16-1x13-0

Family
15-10x15-4

Br 2
12-5x10-0

Porch

Br 3
12-0x10-0

41'-9"

42'-0"

Rear View

To order this plan, visit the Menards Building Materials Desk or visit www.Menards.com.

Plan #M07-007D-0233

Handsome Home For A Narrow Lot

1,298 total square feet of living area

3 bedrooms, 2 baths

2-car garage

Slab foundation

Special features

Open to the great room is the kitchen with snack counter, built-in pantry and convenient adjacent laundry room with coat closet

The breakfast area enjoys lots of windows including a bay with views of the veranda

A luxury bath, walk-in closet, and a patio door with access to the veranda are the many amenities of the master bedroom

Price Code B

Floor plan labels:

38'-0"

54'-8"

Veranda

Brkfst
9-6x10-8

MBr
14-5x11-8

Great Rm
13-0x25-8

Kit
9-3x11-5

R

W
D

Laun

Dining

Br 2
9-0x9-0

Hall

Entry

Garage
18-4x20-4

Br 3
10-8x10-0

Porch

© Copyright by designer/architect

Rear View

To order this plan, visit the Menards Building Materials Desk or visit www.Menards.com.

63

Plan #M07-077L-0138

Delightful Covered Porch

1,509 total square feet of living area

3 bedrooms, 2 baths

2-car garage

Basement, slab or crawl space foundation, please specify when ordering

Special features

A large eating area has covered porch access and is near the kitchen and vaulted great room

Double walk-in closets and a luxury bath complete the master bedroom

Cabinets flank the fireplace in the vaulted great room

Price Code D

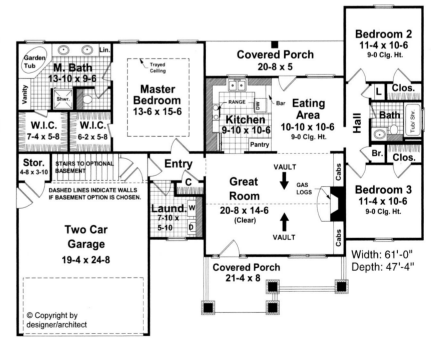

Garden Tub

M. Bath
13-10 x 9-6

Vanity

Lin.

Shwr.

W.I.C.
7-4 x 5-8

W.I.C.
6-2 x 5-8

Stor.
4-8 x 3-10

STAIRS TO OPTIONAL BASEMENT

DASHED LINES INDICATE WALLS IF BASEMENT OPTION IS CHOSEN.

Trayed Ceiling

Master Bedroom
13-6 x 15-6

Entry

C

Laund.
7-10 x 5-10

W
D

Two Car Garage
19-4 x 24-8

© Copyright by designer/architect

Covered Porch
20-8 x 5

RANGE
DW

Kitchen
9-10 x 10-6

Pantry

Bar

Eating Area
10-10 x 10-6
9-0 Clg. Ht.

Cabs

Great Room
20-8 x 14-6
(Clear)

VAULT

GAS LOGS

VAULT

Cabs

Covered Porch
21-4 x 8

Bedroom 2
11-4 x 10-6
9-0 Clg. Ht.

L

Clos.

Hall

Bath

Tub/ Shr.

Br.

Clos.

Bedroom 3
11-4 x 10-6
9-0 Clg. Ht.

Width: 61'-0"
Depth: 47'-4"

Plan #M07-007D-0177

The Ideal Affordable Home

1,102 total square feet of living area

3 bedrooms, 2 baths

2-car garage

Basement foundation, drawings also include slab and crawl space foundations

Special features

The attractive exterior features a cozy porch, pallidian windows and a planter box

The vaulted great room has a fireplace, view to rear patio and dining area with feature window

Open to the great room is a U-shaped kitchen that includes all the necessities including a breakfast bar

The master bedroom offers a vaulted ceiling, private bath, and walk-in closet

Price Code AA

Rear View

Floor plan labels:

38'-0"

51'-8"

Patio

MBr 13-9x12-6 vaulted

Plant Shelf Above

Dn

Great Rm. 17-6x18-6 vaulted

Dine

Hall

Plant Shelf Above

Br 2 10-1x11-0

Br 3 10-0x9-0

Entry

Kit 10-1x9-10 vaulted

DW

R

Porch

Garage 18-8x20-4

© Copyright by designer/architect

To order this plan, visit the Menards Building Materials Desk or visit www.Menards.com.

65

Plan #M07-007D-0088

Country Appeal For A Small Lot

1,299 total square feet of living area

3 bedrooms, 2 1/2 baths

Basement foundation

Special features

First floor master bedroom has a bay window, walk-in closet and roomy bath

Two generous bedrooms with lots of closet space, a hall bath, linen closet and balcony overlook comprise the second floor

Price Code A

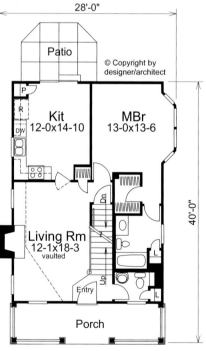

28'-0"

Patio

© Copyright by designer/architect

Kit
12-0x14-10

MBr
13-0x13-6

40'-0"

Living Rm
12-1x18-3
vaulted

Entry

Porch

First Floor
834 sq. ft.

Br 2
12-0x12-6

Br 3
11-0x12-6

Balcony/Hall

Living Rm.
below

Attic

Second Floor
465 sq. ft.

Rear View

To order this plan, visit the Menards Building Materials Desk or visit www.Menards.com.

Menards **Ashridge**

Plan #M07-007D-0103

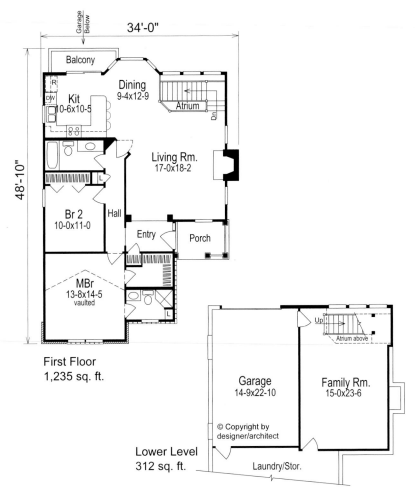

First Floor
1,235 sq. ft.

Garage Below

34'-0"

48'-10"

Balcony

Dining
9-4x12-9

Kit
10-6x10-5

Atrium

Living Rm.
17-0x18-2

Br 2
10-0x11-0

Hall

Entry

Porch

MBr
13-8x14-5
vaulted

Garage
14-9x22-10

Family Rm.
15-0x23-6

Up

Atrium above

© Copyright by
designer/architect

Lower Level
312 sq. ft.

Laundry/Stor.

Atrium Living For Views On A Narrow Lot

1,547 total square feet of living area

2 bedrooms, 2 baths

1-car drive under rear entry garage

Walk-out basement foundation

Special features

Dutch gables and stone accents provide enchanting appearance

The spacious living room offers a masonry fireplace, atrium with window wall and is open to a dining area with bay window

The kitchen has a breakfast counter, cabinet space and glass sliding doors to a balcony

Price Code A

Rear View

Plan #M07-121D-0009

Vaulted Two-Story Great Room

2,205 total square feet of living area

3 bedrooms, 2 1/2 baths

2-car side entry garage

Basement foundation

Special features

The master bedroom enjoys a private first floor location along with an amenity-filled bath and walk-in closet

A flexible loft space can be found on the second floor perfect for a home office or children's play area

The functional kitchen offers an eating bar and a corner walk-in pantry for added storage space

Price Code C

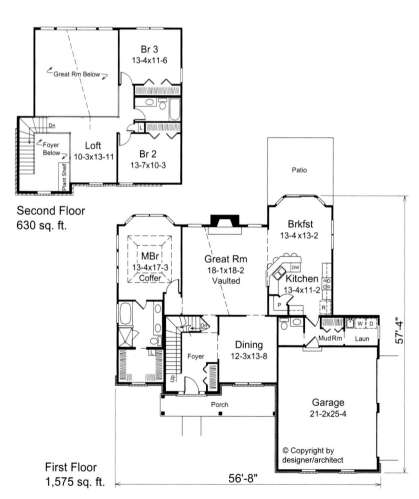

Second Floor
630 sq. ft.

Br 3
13-4x11-6

Great Rm Below

Dn
Foyer Below

Loft
10-3x13-11

Br 2
13-7x10-3

Plant Shelf

First Floor
1,575 sq. ft.

Patio

Brkfst
13-4 x13-2

MBr
13-4x17-3
Coffer

Great Rm
18-1x18-2
Vaulted

Kitchen
13-4x11-2

DW

P

R

57'-4"

Dn

Dining
12-3x13-8

Mud Rm

Laun

W D

Foyer

Up

Garage
21-2x25-4

Porch

© Copyright by designer/architect

56'-8"

Rear View

To order this plan, visit the Menards Building Materials Desk or visit www.Menards.com.

Bay Ranch

Plan #M07-053D-0002

Bay Window Graces Luxury Master Bedroom

1,668 total square feet of living area

3 bedrooms, 2 baths

2-car side entry drive under garage

Walk-out basement foundation

Special features

Large bay windows grace the kitchen/breakfast area, the master bedroom and dining room

Extensive walk-in closets and storage spaces are located throughout the home

Handy covered entry porch

The large living room has a fireplace, built-in bookshelves and a sloped ceiling

Price Code A

Deck

© Copyright by designer/architect

Kit/Brk
11-8x13-6

P

MBr
13-6x13-6
tray clg

Dining
10-0x13-6

Dn

W D

30'-0"

Living
22-0x15-6
sloped ceiling

L

Br 2
11-6x11-8

Br 3
12-6x11-0

Foyer

Porch depth 8-0

54'-0"

Rear View

To order this plan, visit the Menards Building Materials Desk or visit www.Menards.com.

69

Arlington

Plan #M07-001D-0029

Central Fireplace
Warms Family Room

1,260 total square feet of living area

3 bedrooms, 2 baths

2-car garage

Basement foundation, drawings also include crawl space and slab foundations

Special features

The spacious kitchen/dining area features a large pantry, storage area and easy access to the garage and laundry room

A pleasant covered front porch adds a practical touch

The master bedroom with a private bath adjoins two other bedrooms, all with plenty of closet space

Price Code A

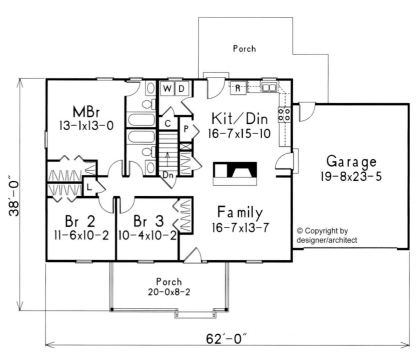

Porch

MBr
13-1x13-0

Kit/Din
16-7x15-10

Garage
19-8x23-5

Family
16-7x13-7

Br 2
11-6x10-2

Br 3
10-4x10-2

© Copyright by
designer/architect

Porch
20-0x8-2

38'-0"

62'-0"

Rear View

To order this plan, visit the Menards Building Materials Desk or visit www.Menards.com.

Plan #M07-008D-0139

Unique A-Frame Detailing Has Appeal

1,272 total square feet of living area

3 bedrooms, 1 1/2 baths

Crawl space foundation

Special features

A stone fireplace accents the living room

The spacious kitchen includes a snack bar overlooking the living room

The first floor bedroom is roomy and secluded

There is plenty of closet space for the second floor bedrooms plus a generous balcony which wraps around the second floor

Price Code A

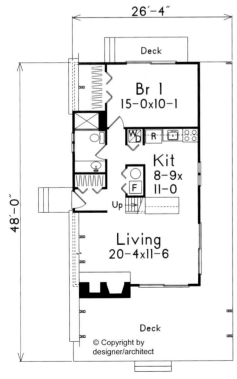

26'-4"

48'-0"

Deck

Br 1
15-0x10-1

W/D   R

Kit
8-9x
11-0

F

Up

Living
20-4x11-6

Deck

© Copyright by designer/architect

First Floor
792 sq. ft.

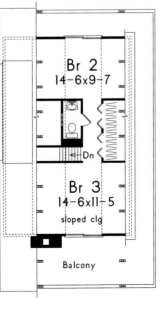

Br 2
14-6x9-7

Dn

Br 3
14-6x11-5
sloped clg

Balcony

Second Floor
480 sq. ft.

Plan #M07-007D-0200

Especially Designed For A Small Lot

1,137 total square feet of living area

2 bedrooms, 1 1/2 baths

2-car garage

Walk-out basement foundation

Special features

Cleverly designed two-story is disguised as an attractive one-story home

The living room with fireplace is open to the bayed dining area and L-shaped kitchen

The optional finished lower level includes a family room, hall bath and third bedroom and allows for an extra 591 square feet of living area

Price Code A

Rear View

First Floor
621 sq. ft.

Second Floor
516 sq. ft.

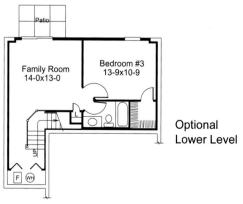

Optional
Lower Level

To order this plan, visit the *Menards* Building Materials Desk or visit *www.Menards.com*.

Plan #M07-033D-0013

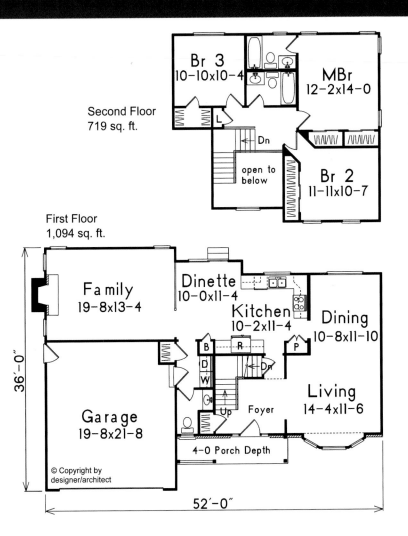

Second Floor
719 sq. ft.

Br 3
10-10x10-4

MBr
12-2x14-0

Dn

open to
below

Br 2
11-11x10-7

First Floor
1,094 sq. ft.

Family
19-8x13-4

Dinette
10-0x11-4

Kitchen
10-2x11-4

Dining
10-8x11-10

B

R

D

W

P

Up

Foyer

Living
14-4x11-6

Garage
19-8x21-8

36'-0"

© Copyright by
designer/architect

4-0 Porch Depth

52'-0"

Great Plan For Formal And Informal Entertaining

1,813 total square feet of living area

3 bedrooms, 2 1/2 baths

2-car garage

Basement foundation

Special features

The bedrooms are located on the second floor for privacy

The living room with large bay window joins the dining room for expansive formal entertaining

The family room, dinette and kitchen combine for an impressive living area

The two-story foyer and L-shaped staircase create a dramatic entry

Inviting covered porch greets guests

Price Code D

Rear View

To order this plan, visit the Menards Building Materials Desk or visit www.Menards.com.

73

Rosencrest

Plan #M07-077L-0074

Shutters Add Style
To The Exterior

1,502 total square feet of living area

3 bedrooms, 2 baths

2-car side entry garage

Crawl space or slab foundation, please specify when ordering

Special features

The dining area or sunroom is open and airy with windows all around and includes a 9' ceiling and patio access

The kitchen features raised bars facing the dining and living rooms

The gas fireplace makes the living room a warm, friendly place to gather

Price Code D

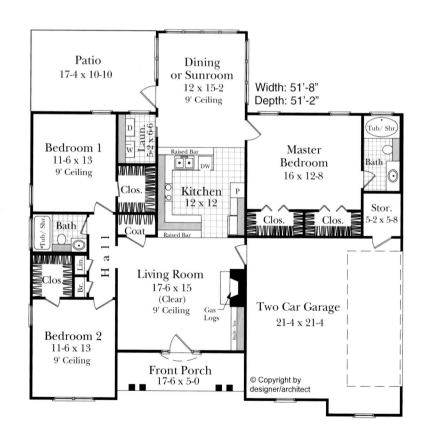

Patio
17-4 x 10-10

Dining
or Sunroom
12 x 15-2
9' Ceiling

Width: 51'-8"
Depth: 51'-2"

Bedroom 1
11-6 x 13
9' Ceiling

Laun.
5-2 x 6-6

D
W

Raised Bar

DW

Kitchen
12 x 12

Master
Bedroom
16 x 12-8

Tub/Shr.

Bath

Clos.

Coat

Clos.

Raised Bar

P

Clos.

Clos.

Stor.
5-2 x 5-8

Tub/Shr.

Bath

Clos.

Br.

Lin.

Hall

Living Room
17-6 x 15
(Clear)
9' Ceiling

Gas
Logs

Built-In

Two Car Garage
21-4 x 21-4

Bedroom 2
11-6 x 13
9' Ceiling

Front Porch
17-6 x 5-0

© Copyright by
designer/architect

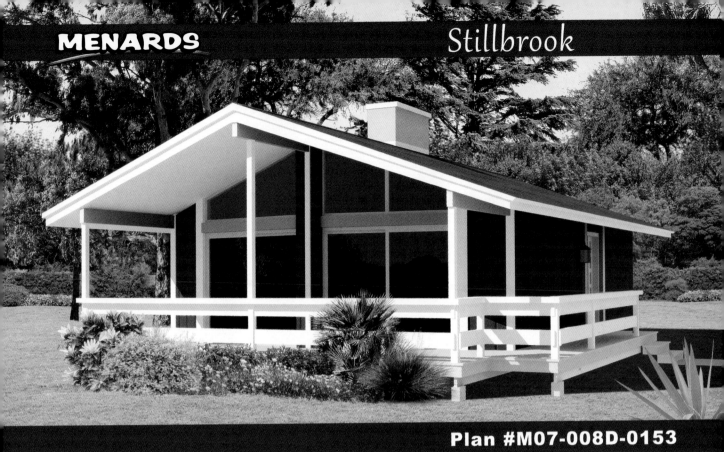

Plan #M07-008D-0153

Great Views From The Covered Deck

792 total square feet of living area

2 bedrooms, 1 bath

Crawl space foundation, drawings also include slab foundation

Special features

The attractive exterior features wood posts and beams, wrap-around deck with railing and sliding glass doors with transoms

The kitchen, living and dining areas enjoy sloped ceilings, a cozy fireplace and views over the deck

Two bedrooms share a bath just off the hall

Price Code AAA

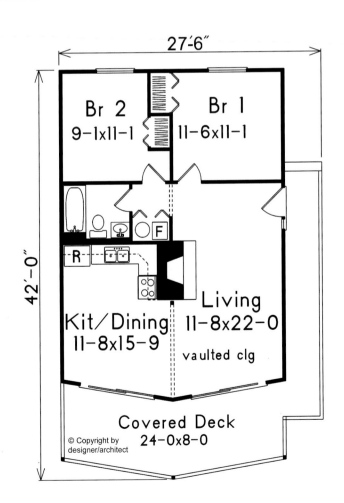

27'-6"

42'-0"

Br 2
9-1x11-1

Br 1
11-6x11-1

R

F

Kit/Dining
11-8x15-9

Living
11-8x22-0

vaulted clg

Covered Deck
24-0x8-0

© Copyright by designer/architect

To order this plan, visit the Menards Building Materials Desk or visit www.Menards.com.

75

Sumner

Plan #M07-013L-0028

Casual Farmhouse Appeal

2,239 total square feet of living area

3 bedrooms, 2 1/2 baths

2-car detached garage

Basement or crawl space foundation, please specify when ordering

Special features

Two sets of French doors in the family room lead to a rear covered porch ideal for relaxing

The master bedroom has a spacious bath with an oversized tub placed in a sunny bay window

Both second floor bedrooms have storage closets for terrific organizing

Price Code D

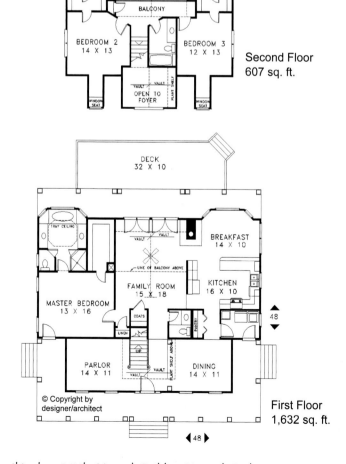

Second Floor
607 sq. ft.

First Floor
1,632 sq. ft.

Delta Queen II

Plan #M07-001D-0068

Layout Creates
Large Open Living Area

1,285 total square feet of living area

3 bedrooms, 2 baths

Crawl space foundation, drawings also include basement and slab foundations

Special features

A large storage area can be found on the back of the home

The master bedroom includes a dressing area, private bath and built-in bookcase

The kitchen features a pantry, breakfast bar and complete view to the dining room

2" x 6" exterior walls available, please order plan #M07-001D-0120

Price Code B

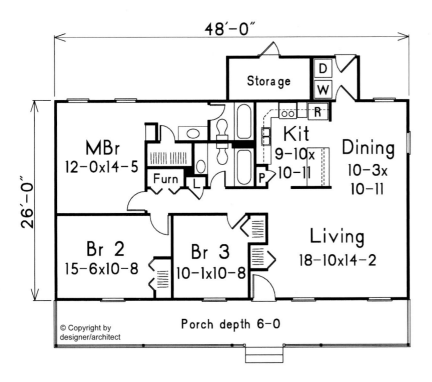

48'-0"

26'-0"

Storage

D
W
R

MBr
12-0x14-5

Furn   L

Kit
9-10x
10-11

P

Dining
10-3x
10-11

Br 2
15-6x10-8

Br 3
10-1x10-8

Living
18-10x14-2

© Copyright by designer/architect

Porch depth 6-0

Rear View

To order this plan, visit the Menards Building Materials Desk or visit www.Menards.com.

77

Plan #M07-010D-0007

Large Windows Grace This Split-Level Home

1,427 total square feet of living area

3 bedrooms, 2 baths

2-car drive under garage

Basement foundation

Special features

Practical storage space is situated in the garage

A convenient laundry closet is located on the lower level

The kitchen and dining area both have sliding doors that access the deck

A large expansive space is created by the vaulted living and dining rooms

Price Code A

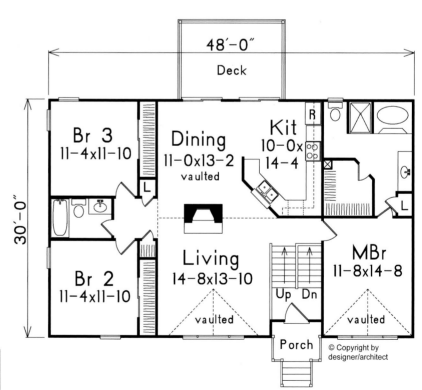

Deck — 48'-0"

30'-0"

Br 3
11-4x11-10

Dining
11-0x13-2
vaulted

Kit
10-0x
14-4

R

L

L

Br 2
11-4x11-10

Living
14-8x13-10
vaulted

Up Dn

MBr
11-8x14-8
vaulted

Porch

© Copyright by
designer/architect

Rear View

To order this plan, visit the Menards Building Materials Desk or visit www.Menards.com.

Plan #M07-055L-0100

Second Floor
322 sq. ft.

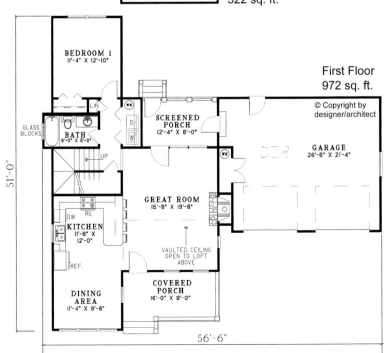

First Floor
972 sq. ft.

© Copyright by
designer/architect

Screened Porch For Outdoor Enjoyment

1,294 total square feet of living area

2 bedrooms, 2 baths

2-car garage

Crawl space or slab foundation, please specify when ordering

Special features

Second floor bedroom #2/loft has its own bath and a vaulted ceiling overlooking the great room below

The great room has a cozy fireplace and accesses both the front and the rear of the home

The laundry area on the first floor is convenient to the kitchen

Price Code A

To order this plan, visit the Menards Building Materials Desk or visit www.Menards.com.

79

Plan #M07-024L-0350

Appealing Front Entry

2,011 total square feet of living area

3 bedrooms, 2 1/2 baths

2-car side entry carport

Slab foundation

Special features

The open second floor study can serve as an office or homework station located away from the busier portions of the home

The kitchen peninsula is a casual place to grab a snack while providing an uninhibited view into the great room

A double-bowl vanity in the master bath ensures everyone has their own space when it is time to prepare for the day ahead

Price Code C

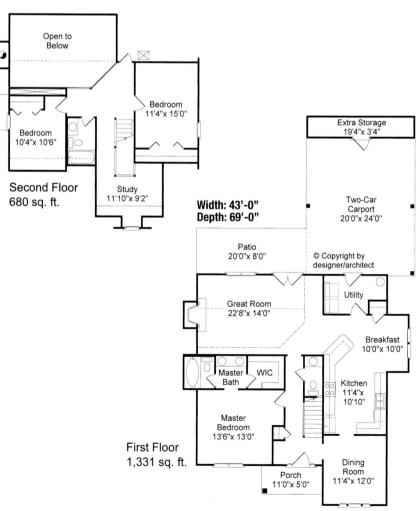

Open to Below

Bedroom
10'4"x 10'6"

Bedroom
11'4"x 15'0"

Study
11'10"x 9'2"

Second Floor
680 sq. ft.

Width: 43'-0"
Depth: 69'-0"

Extra Storage
19'4"x 3'4"

Two-Car Carport
20'0"x 24'0"

© Copyright by designer/architect

Patio
20'0"x 8'0"

Great Room
22'8"x 14'0"

Utility

Breakfast
10'0"x 10'0"

Master Bath

WIC

Kitchen
11'4"x 10'10"

Master Bedroom
13'6"x 13'0"

First Floor
1,331 sq. ft.

Porch
11'0"x 5'0"

Dining Room
11'4"x 12'0"

To order this plan, visit the Menards Building Materials Desk or visit www.Menards.com.

Plan #M07-008D-0085

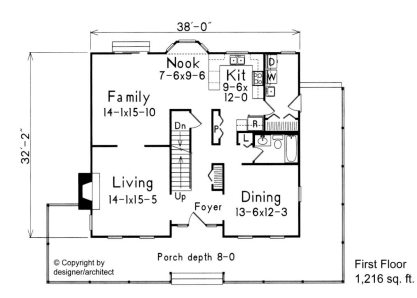

Second Floor
896 sq. ft.

Br 3
12-9x12-7

MBr
14-1x17-7
vaulted

skylt

Dn

Br 2
13-6x11-8
vaulted

open to below

38'-0"

32'-2"

Nook
7-6x9-6

Kit
9-6x
12-0

Family
14-1x15-10

Dn

Living
14-1x15-5

Up

Foyer

Dining
13-6x12-3

© Copyright by
designer/architect

Porch depth 8-0

First Floor
1,216 sq. ft.

Attractive Dormers Enhance Facade

2,112 total square feet of living area

3 bedrooms, 3 baths

Basement foundation, drawings
also include crawl space foundation

Special features

The kitchen efficiently connects to the formal
dining area

A bayed nook is located between the family
room and kitchen creating an ideal breakfast
area

The vaulted master bedroom features a
skylight, walk-in closet and private bath

Price Code C

To order this plan, visit the *Menards* Building Materials Desk or visit *www.Menards.com*.

81

Plan #M07-040D-0006

Well-Sculptured Design, Inside And Out

1,759 total square feet of living area

3 bedrooms, 2 1/2 baths

2-car garage

Basement foundation

Special features

The striking entry is created by a unique staircase layout, an open high ceiling and a fireplace

The second floor bedrooms share a private dressing area and bath

The bonus area over the garage, that is included in the square footage, could easily convert to a fourth bedroom or activity center

Price Code B

Rear View

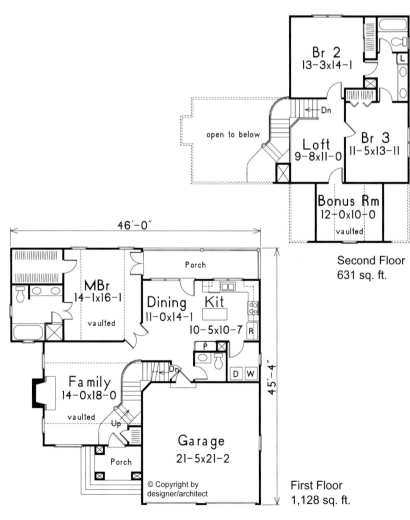

Second Floor
631 sq. ft.

First Floor
1,128 sq. ft.

© Copyright by designer/architect

To order this plan, visit the Menards Building Materials Desk or visit www.Menards.com.

Plan #M07-055L-0188

Bayed Dining Room

1,525 total square feet of living area

3 bedrooms, 2 baths

2-car garage

Slab, crawl space, basement or walk-out basement foundation, please specify when ordering

Special features

The kitchen is enhanced with an open bar that connects to the great room

A corner gas fireplace warms the entire living area

The master suite features a whirlpool tub flanked by walk-in closets

Price Code C

[Floor plan drawing]

51'-6"

WHP TUB

M.BATH
15'-8" X 10'-8"

LIN

COVERED PORCH
24'-10" X 9'-8"

ATRIUM DOOR

GRILLING PATIO
10'-4" X 9'-8"

DINING ROOM
11'-0" X 9'-6"

GAS FIREPLACE

MASTER SUITE
15'-8" X 12'-0"
9' BOXED CEILING

OPEN BAR

BRKFAST ROOM
10'-0" X 8'-0"

COMPUTER DESK

GREAT ROOM
13'-6" X 19'-8"
9' BOXED CEILING

KITCHEN
15'-2" X 10'-8"
REF

RG

BATH

DW

LAU.
6'-4" X 5'-6"

WH

D

W

49'-10"

OPT DOOR

LIN

GARAGE
20'-10" X 20'-0"

FOYER
6'-8" X 7'-0"

BEDROOM 3 STUDY
10'-0" X 10'-8"

BEDROOM 2
10'-2" X 10'-8"

© Copyright by designer/architect

COVERED PORCH
16'-5" X 5'-0"

To order this plan, visit the *Menards Building Materials Desk* or visit www.Menards.com.

83

Ivy

MENARDS

Plan #M07-017D-0002

Farmhouse Style
Offers Great Privacy

1,805 total square feet of living area

3 bedrooms, 2 1/2 baths

2-car side entry garage

Basement foundation, drawings also include slab foundation

Special features

Energy efficient home with 2" x 6" exterior walls

The master bedroom forms its own wing

The second floor bedrooms share a hall bath

The large great room with fireplace blends into the formal dining room

Price Code D

Rear View

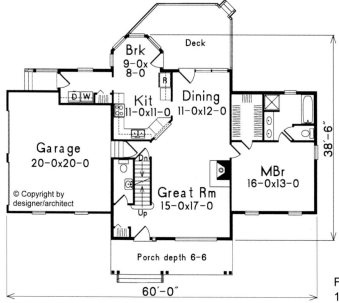

Br 3
12-2x14-4

Attic

Dn

Attic

Br 2
15-0x14-0

Second Floor
560 sq. ft.

Brk
9-0x
8-0

Deck

DW

Kit
11-0x11-0

Dining
11-0x12-0

Garage
20-0x20-0

© Copyright by
designer/architect

Dn

Great Rm
15-0x17-0

Up

MBr
16-0x13-0

38'-6"

Porch depth 6-6

60'-0"

First Floor
1,245 sq. ft.

84   To order this plan, visit the Menards Building Materials Desk or visit www.Menards.com.

Rebecca

Plan #M07-121D-0015

Welcoming Covered Front Porch

1,983 total square feet of living area

3 bedrooms, 2 1/2 baths

2-car side entry garage

Basement foundation

Special features

The vaulted great room offers a fireplace and a wall of windows to brighten the space

The master bath has a separate toilet room, double-bowl vanity and large walk-in closet

Bedrooms #2 and #3 share a bath

The optional attic space above the garage has an additional 273 square feet of living area

Price Code B

Floor plan labels:

60'-0"
61'-0"

Patio

MBr 14-9x16-8 Coffer

Brkfst 12-3x10-0 Vaulted

Kitchen 12-3x10-5 Vaulted

Great Rm 17-7x20-1 Vaulted

Br 2 11-5x11-4

Br 3 11-5x11-1

Dining 11-6x11-1 13' Clg

Laun/Mud Rm

Entry

Porch

Garage 22-10x24-8

Opt. Attic Space

© Copyright by designer/architect

Rear View

To order this plan, visit the Menards Building Materials Desk or visit www.Menards.com.

85

Carmel Valley

Plan #M07-039L-0027

Wonderful Two-Story Home

1,612 total square feet of living area

3 bedrooms, 2 1/2 baths

2-car garage

Basement foundation

Special features

A private master bedroom offers all the essentials for everyday living

A delightful family room with fireplace is ideally suited for casual family gatherings

Well-planned design enjoys a center island in the kitchen

Price Code C

Second Floor
485 sq. ft.

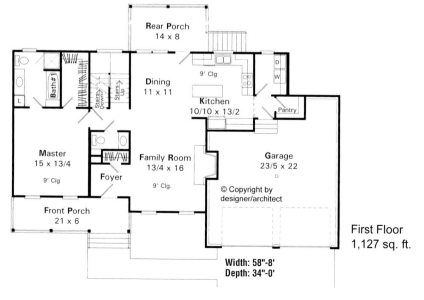

First Floor
1,127 sq. ft.

Width: 58"-8'
Depth: 34'-0'

Mstr Bedrm
13-2x15-4

Bedrm 3
10-8x11-5

Bedrm 2
14-1x11-4

Second Floor
804 sq. ft.

58'-0"

30'-8"

Family Rm
16-1x12-1

Kitchen
11-1x12-1

DW R

Mud Rm

Garage
21-8x21-4

Living Rm
13-1x17-7

Foyer

Bedrm/Dining
13-1x12-4

© Copyright by
designer/architect

First Floor
1,068 sq. ft.

Design Has Traditional Elegance

1,872 total square feet of living area

4 bedrooms, 2 baths

2-car garage

Basement foundation, drawings also include crawl space and slab foundations

Special features

The recessed porch has an entry door with sidelights and roof dormers adding charm

The foyer with handcrafted staircase adjoins the living room with fireplace

The first floor bedroom/dining has access to the bath and laundry room making it perfect for a live-in parent retreat

The master bedroom on the second floor enjoys double closets and private access to the hall bath

Price Code C

Harrison Glen

Plan #M07-013L-0045

Efficiently Designed Two-Story

1,695 total square feet of living area

3 bedrooms, 3 baths

2-car garage

Basement foundation

Special features

The large family room with fireplace makes a spacious, yet cozy gathering place

The garage has a convenient workshop space in the back

The screened porch offers protection from the sun and insects and connects to the open deck

The bonus room above the garage has an additional 290 square feet of living area

Price Code C

Second Floor
816 sq. ft.

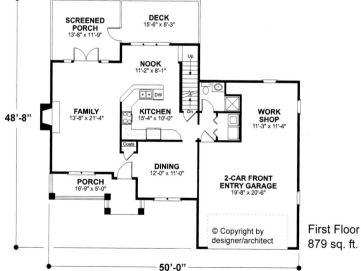

First Floor
879 sq. ft.

Plan #M07-008D-0026

Lovely Inviting Covered Porch

1,120 total square feet of living area

3 bedrooms, 1 bath

1-car carport

Basement foundation, drawings also include crawl space and slab foundations

Special features

The family room/kitchen creates a useful spacious area

The rustic, colonial design is perfect for many surroundings

An oversized living room is ideal for entertaining

The carport includes a functional storage area

The optional master bath can be converted to a closet for extra storage

Price Code AA

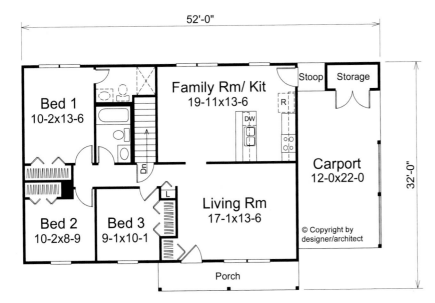

To order this plan, visit the Menards Building Materials Desk or visit www.Menards.com.

89

MENARDS

Plan #M07-058D-0073

Ideal Home Or Retirement Retreat

1,013 total square feet of living area

2 bedrooms, 1 bath

Slab foundation

Special features

Energy efficient home with 2" x 6" exterior walls

Vaulted ceilings can be found in both the family room and kitchen with a dining area just beyond the breakfast bar

The plant shelf above the kitchen cabinetry is a special feature

The oversized utility room has space for a full-size washer and dryer

A hall bath is centrally located with easy access from both bedrooms

Price Code AA

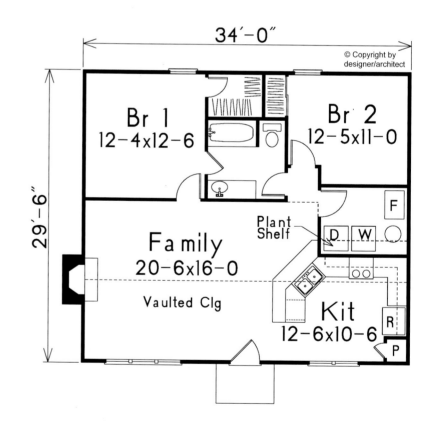

© Copyright by designer/architect

34'-0"

29'-6"

Br 1
12-4x12-6

Br 2
12-5x11-0

Family
20-6x16-0

Vaulted Clg

Plant Shelf

F

D W

Kit
12-6x10-6

R

P

To order this plan, visit the *Menards* Building Materials Desk or visit www.Menards.com.

MENARDS
Cottage
HOME PLANS

Plan #M07-055L-0530 on page 94.

Cottage Home Plans is a collection of our best-selling charming cottage homes in a variety of architectural styles from rustic to Victorian. Exuding charm from years gone by, these homes offer old-fashioned style while providing all the modern conveniences active families want today. Take a trip to the past and browse these nostalgic cottage plans.

Plan #M07-007D-0105 on page 98.

Plan #M07-007D-0201 on page 127.

Cottage Home Plans

Plan #M07-055L-0350

Photo, above - Gracious and warm, the den provides an inviting atmosphere full of warmth and casual country comfort.

Photo, left - Plenty of cabinetry and counterspace line the U-shaped kitchen offering an abundance of storage while also keeping everything efficiently within reach when cooking and preparing meals.

Photo, above - The fireplace commands full attention in the comfortable surroundings of the den. No doubt its warmth will be felt throughout the interior of the first floor of this home and especially the adjacent dining room.

Photo, right - Simple country style living is perfectly displayed in this modest bedroom.

Plan #M07-055L-0350

Country Cottage For A Narrow Lot

1,451 total square feet of living area

3 bedrooms, 2 baths

Slab or crawl space foundation, please specify when ordering

Special features

A cozy atmosphere is achieved in the den with a prominent stone fireplace

An 8' deep covered front porch encourages outdoor relaxation and enjoyment

Two secondary bedrooms with dormers share a full bath

Price Code B

Second Floor
583 sq. ft.

First Floor
868 sq. ft.

© Copyright by designer/architect

To order this plan, visit the Menards Building Materials Desk.

Cottage Home Plans

Plan #M07-055L-0530

Bungalow Home With Stylish Roof Dormers

2,237 total square feet of living area

3 bedrooms, 2 1/2 baths

2-car rear entry garage

Crawl space or slab foundation, please specify when ordering

Special features

The stunning open great room has a center fireplace and a corner wet bar with sink and refrigerator

The private master bath includes a large corner whirlpool tub and a separate shower plus a large walk-in closet for organization

The peninsula in the kitchen features enough casual dining space for two people to comfortably dine

Price Code D

First Floor
1,708 sq. ft.

Second Floor
529 sq. ft.

Rear View

To order this plan, visit the Menards Building Materials Desk or visit www.Menards.com.

Plan #M07-001D-0036

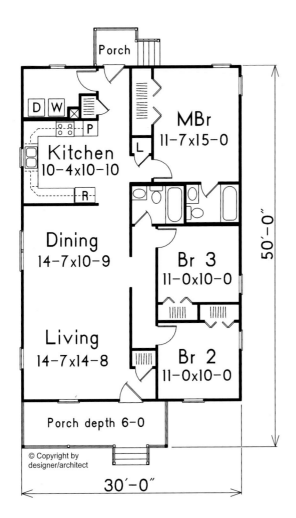

Porch

D W
P
Kitchen
10-4x10-10
R

MBr
11-7x15-0
L

Dining
14-7x10-9

Br 3
11-0x10-0

Living
14-7x14-8

Br 2
11-0x10-0

Porch depth 6-0

© Copyright by
designer/architect

50'-0"

30'-0"

Gabled, Covered Front Porch

1,320 total square feet of living area

3 bedrooms, 2 baths

Crawl space foundation

Special features

A functional U-shaped kitchen features a pantry

Large living and dining areas join to create an open atmosphere

The secluded master bedroom includes a private full bath

The covered front porch opens into a large living area with a convenient coat closet

The utility/laundry room is located near the kitchen

Price Code A

Rear View

To order this plan, visit the Menards Building Materials Desk or visit www.Menards.com.

95

Haverhill

MENARDS

Plan #M07-040D-0028

Cottage Style 1s
Appealing And Cozy

828 total square feet of living area

2 bedrooms, 1 bath

Crawl space foundation

Special features

The vaulted ceiling in the family room enhances space

The convenient laundry room is located near the rear entry

There is efficient storage space under the stairs

A covered entry porch provides a cozy sitting area and plenty of shade

Price Code AAA

Rear View

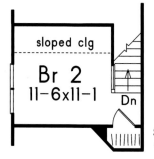

sloped clg

Br 2
11-6x11-1

Dn

Second Floor
168 sq. ft.

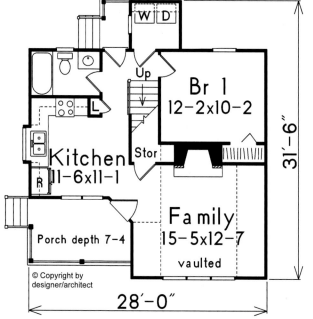

W D

Up

Br 1
12-2x10-2

L

Kitchen
11-6x11-1

R

Stor

31'-6"

Porch depth 7-4

Family
15-5x12-7

vaulted

© Copyright by designer/architect

28'-0"

First Floor
660 sq. ft.

To order this plan, visit the Menards Building Materials Desk or visit www.Menards.com.

Plan #M07-055L-0526

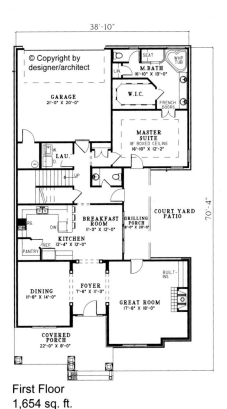

First Floor
1,654 sq. ft.

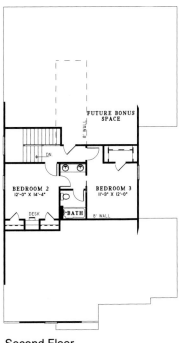

Second Floor
492 sq. ft.

Classic Tudor Features Highlight This Craftsman Home

2,146 total square feet of living area

3 bedrooms, 2 1/2 baths

2-car rear entry garage

Crawl space or slab foundation, please specify when ordering

Special features

The extended counter in the kitchen features enough casual dining space for three people to comfortably dine

The stunning great room has a center fireplace and direct access to the grilling porch

The private master bath includes both a large corner whirlpool tub and a separate shower

Price Code D

To order this plan, visit the Menards Building Materials Desk or visit www.Menards.com.

97

Plan #M07-007D-0105

Stylish Retreat For A Narrow Lot

1,084 total square feet of living area

2 bedrooms, 2 baths

Basement foundation

Special features

The living room offers a front feature window which invites the sun and includes a fireplace and dining area with patio

The U-shaped kitchen features lots of cabinets and a bayed breakfast room with built-in pantry

Both bedrooms have walk-in closets and access to their own bath

Price Code AA

Rear View

To order this plan, visit the Menards Building Materials Desk or visit www.Menards.com.

MENARDS

Woodsmill

Plan #M07-007D-0042

30'-0"

33'-0"

Br 2
11-0x9-7

Kit
11-0x8-0

R | DW

P

Deck

Dn

Hall

Dn

Dining

MBr
11-0x12-0

Living
12-7x19-4

Dn

Entry

© Copyright by designer/architect

Porch

First Floor
796 sq. ft.

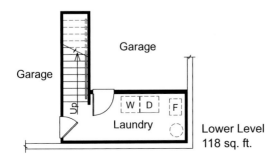

Garage

Garage

Up

W | D | F

Laundry

Lower Level
118 sq. ft.

Small Home Is Remarkably Spacious

914 total square feet of living area

2 bedrooms, 1 bath

2-car drive under rear entry garage

Basement foundation

Special features

Large porch for leisurely evenings

The dining area with bay window, open stairs and a pass-through kitchen create openness

The basement includes generous garage space, a storage area, finished laundry and mechanical room

Price Code AA

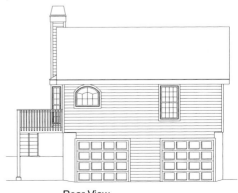

Rear View

To order this plan, visit the Menards Building Materials Desk or visit www.Menards.com.

99

Cottage Home Plans

Plan #M07-058D-0004

Country Cottage Offers A Large Vaulted Living Space

962 total square feet of living area

2 bedrooms, 1 bath

Crawl space foundation

Special features

Both the kitchen and family room share warmth from the fireplace

The charming facade features a covered porch on one side, screened porch on the other and attractive planter boxes

An L-shaped kitchen boasts a convenient pantry

Price Code AA

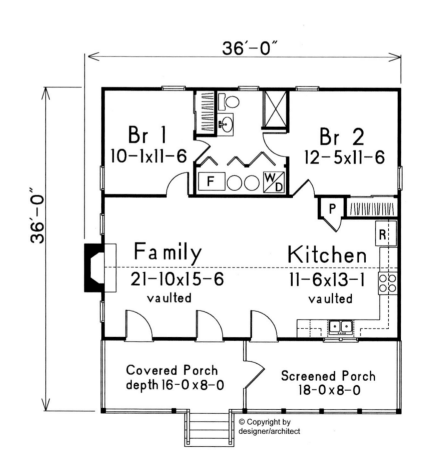

Br 1
10-1x11-6

Br 2
12-5x11-6

F

W D

Family
21-10x15-6
vaulted

Kitchen
11-6x13-1
vaulted

P

R

36'-0"

36'-0"

Covered Porch
depth 16-0 x 8-0

Screened Porch
18-0 x 8-0

© Copyright by designer/architect

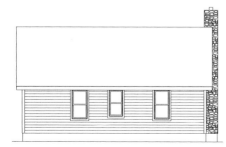

Rear View

To order this plan, visit the Menards Building Materials Desk or visit www.Menards.com.

Plan #M07-013L-0132

Cheerful Narrow Lot Home

2,296 total square feet of living area

3 bedrooms, 3 1/2 baths

2-car garage

Crawl space foundation

Special features

The highly functional kitchen offers double snack bars, a pantry and an adjacent breakfast nook

Located off of the breakfast nook is an oversized laundry room with plenty of space for a washer and dryer as well as a laundry sink and upright freezer

The spacious master bedroom, with its bowed window, tray ceiling, sitting area, luxurious bath and abundant closet, is truly an owner's retreat

The second floor features two secondary bedroom suites, each featuring a walk-in closet and private bath

Price Code F

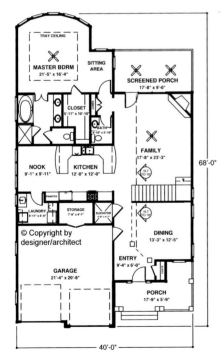

First Floor
1,636 sq. ft.

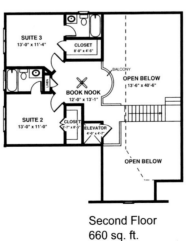

Second Floor
660 sq. ft.

To order this plan, visit the Menards Building Materials Desk or visit www.Menards.com.

101

Plan #M07-072L-0058

Craftsman Style Cottage

1,800 total square feet of living area

3 bedrooms, 2 baths

2-car rear entry garage

Basement foundation

Special features

Suited for a narrow lot, this bungalow offers tremendous curb appeal and a stylish interior

An entire wall of windows adds a generous amount of sunlight to the family room

The master bedroom is separated from the other bedrooms and also enjoys a private bath with shower and whirlpool tub

Price Code D

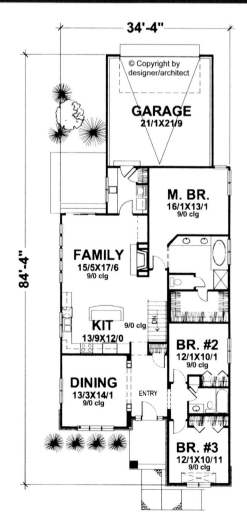

Plan #M07-007D-0175

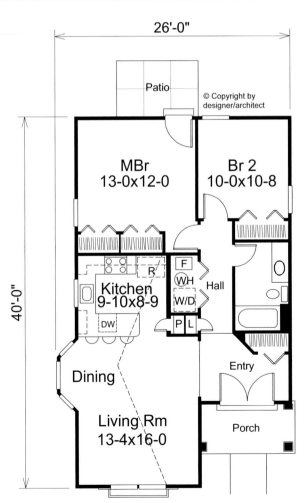

26'-0"

Patio

© Copyright by
designer/architect

MBr
13-0x12-0

Br 2
10-0x10-8

40'-0"

Kitchen
9-10x8-9

F
WH
W/D
P L

Hall

DW

Dining

Entry

Living Rm
13-4x16-0

Porch

Stylish Cottage Home

882 total square feet of living area

2 bedrooms, 1 bath

Crawl space foundation, drawings also
include slab and basement foundations

Special features

An inviting porch and entry lure the owners
and guests into this warm and cozy home

Living room features a vaulted ceiling, bayed
dining area and is open to a well-equipped
U-shaped kitchen

The master bedroom has two separate
closets and patio access

Price Code AAA

Rear View

To order this plan, visit the *Menards* Building Materials Desk or visit www.Menards.com.

103

Plan #M07-024L-0140

Ideal Home To Tackle A Narrow Lot

1,612 total square feet of living area

3 bedrooms, 2 baths

Slab foundation

Special features

The expansive living room has a corner fireplace that warms the entire area and a back door that leads to the covered porch

The sparkling master bedroom offers homeowners a bath with a pampering whirlpool tub, a double-bowl vanity for convenience and a large walk-in closet

Charming amenities in the kitchen include a generously sized pantry, dual sinks and an efficient dishwasher

Price Code C

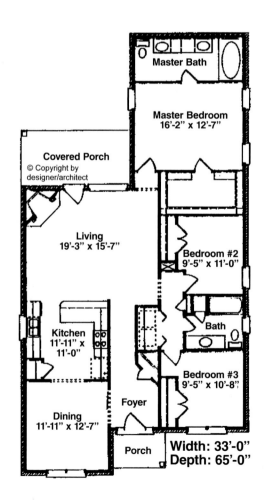

Master Bath

Master Bedroom
16'-2" x 12'-7"

Covered Porch
© Copyright by
designer/architect

Living
19'-3" x 15'-7"

Bedroom #2
9'-5" x 11'-0"

Bath

Kitchen
11'-11" x 11'-0"

Bedroom #3
9'-5" x 10'-8"

Foyer

Dining
11'-11" x 12'-7"

Porch

Width: 33'-0"
Depth: 65'-0"

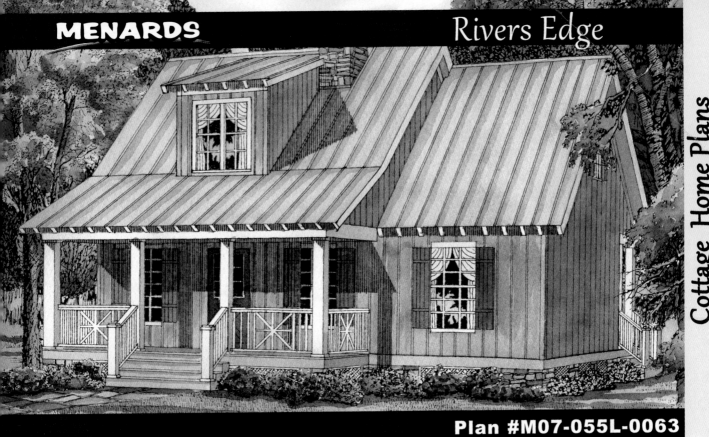

Plan #M07-055L-0063

Second Floor
507 sq. ft.

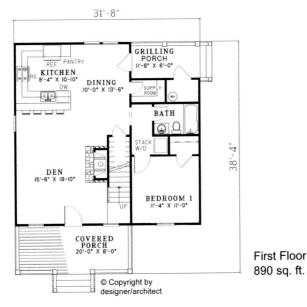

First Floor
890 sq. ft.

© Copyright by
designer/architect

Sportsman's Paradise Cabin

1,397 total square feet of living area

3 bedrooms, 2 baths

Crawl space or slab foundation,
please specify when ordering

Special features

The den with rock hearth fireplace opens to
dining area and kitchen

The kitchen and dining area have an eat-in
bar with access to a rear grilling porch

The second floor bedrooms have unique
ceilings and lots of closet space

Price Code A

To order this plan, visit the Menards Building Materials Desk or visit www.Menards.com.

105

Waltham Forest

MENARDS

Plan #M07-007D-0218

Classic English Tudor Home

1,828 total square feet of living area

3 bedrooms, 2 1/2 baths

2-car garage

Crawl space foundation

Special features

The first floor bedroom and full bath are the answer to overnight guests, a child home from college or a visiting in-law

A 20' x 13' unfinished room behind the garage is ideal for a workshop, office, art studio, family room, game room or expanding any way you wish

The second floor has a large master bedroom with two walk-in closets, a luxury bath, 9' wide patio doors to a private outdoor balcony

Price Code C

Rear View

Second Floor
704 sq. ft.

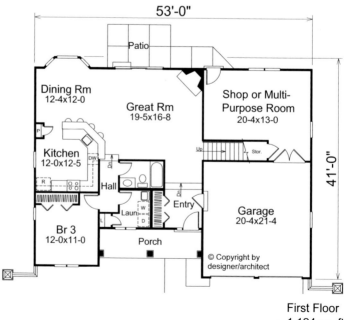

First Floor
1,124 sq. ft.

To order this plan, visit the Menards Building Materials Desk or visit www.Menards.com.

Plan #M07-055L-0066

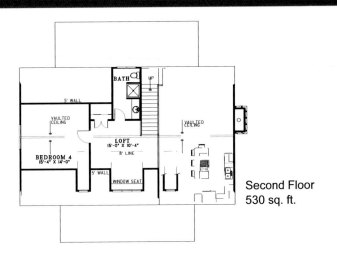

Second Floor
530 sq. ft.

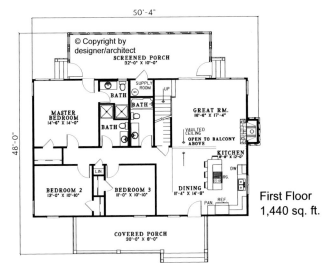

First Floor
1,440 sq. ft.

Covered Porch Adds Charm

1,970 total square feet of living area

4 bedrooms, 4 baths

Crawl space or slab foundation,
please specify when ordering

Special features

30' x 8' covered front porch

The great room has a vaulted ceiling
and fireplace

The master bedroom features access to
the rear screened porch for convenience

Bedroom #4 has a vaulted ceiling and
access to loft with window seat

Price Code B

Cottage Home Plans

Plan #M07-058D-0010

Small And Cozy Cabin

676 total square feet of living area

1 bedroom, 1 bath

Crawl space foundation

Special features

A see-through fireplace between the bedroom and living area adds character

Combined dining and living areas create an open feeling

The full-length front covered porch is perfect for enjoying the outdoors

2" x 6" exterior walls available, please order plan #M07-058D-0074

Price Code AAA

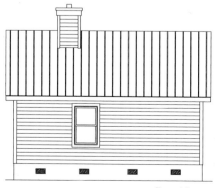

Rear View

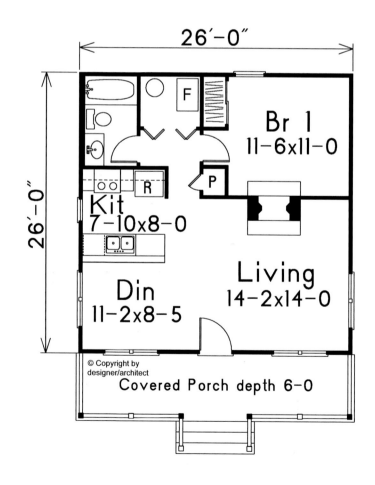

26'-0"

26'-0"

Br 1
11-6x11-0

Kit
7-10x8-0

F

P

R

Din
11-2x8-5

Living
14-2x14-0

© Copyright by
designer/architect

Covered Porch depth 6-0

To order this plan, visit the *Menards* Building Materials Desk or visit *www.Menards.com.*

Plan #M07-007D-0142

Cozy Retreat For Weekends

480 total square feet of living area

1 bedroom, 1 bath

1-car garage

Slab foundation

Special features

An inviting wrap-around porch and rear covered patio are perfect for summer evenings

The living room features a fireplace, separate entry foyer with coat closet and sliding doors to a rear patio

The compact, but complete kitchen includes a dining area with bay window and a window at the sink for patio views

Price Code AAA

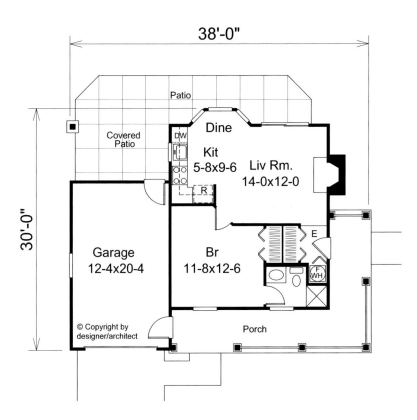

Rear View

To order this plan, visit the *Menards Building Materials Desk* or visit www.Menards.com.

109

Plan #M07-055L-0069

Cozy Cabin With Open Floor Plan

1,400 total square feet of living area

2 bedrooms, 2 baths

Crawl space or slab foundation, please specify when ordering

Special features

A front covered porch leads into the great room

The great room features a vaulted ceiling and fireplace for warmth

The rear grilling porch includes a practical and convenient supply room

Price Code A

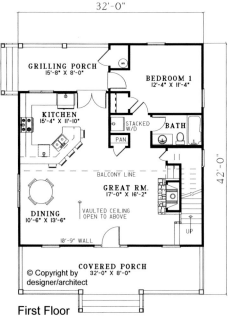

First Floor
948 sq. ft.

Second Floor
452 sq. ft.

Plan #M07-007D-0196

Comfortable And Cozy Cottage

421 total square feet of living area

1 bedroom, 1 bath

1-car garage

Slab foundation

Special features

A recessed porch for protection from inclement weather adds charm to the exterior

The living room features a large bay window, convenient kitchenette and an entry area with guest closet

A full size bath and closet are provided for the bedroom

Price Code AAA

27'-0"

27'-0"

Bedroom
12-0x8-6

Garage
12-0x20-4

Liv. Rm./Kit.
14-0x12-1

R

Entry

Porch

F/WH

© Copyright by designer/architect

Rear View

To order this plan, visit the Menards Building Materials Desk or visit www.Menards.com.

111

Cuddington Forest

MENARDS

Cottage Home Plans

Plan #M07-007D-0238

Narrow Lot Old World Charm

2,250 total square feet of living area

3 bedrooms, 2 1/2 baths

2-car garage

Basement foundation

Special features

The living room with fireplace enjoys an adjacent entry foyer, guest closet and large separate dining area with access to the patio

A snack bar, center island and walk-in pantry are a few amenities of the kitchen

The breakfast area, open to the kitchen, has an interesting curved wall and glass sliding doors to the rear patio

The finished closet space on the lower level is 134 square feet and is included in the total square footage

Price Code E

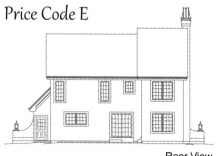

Rear View

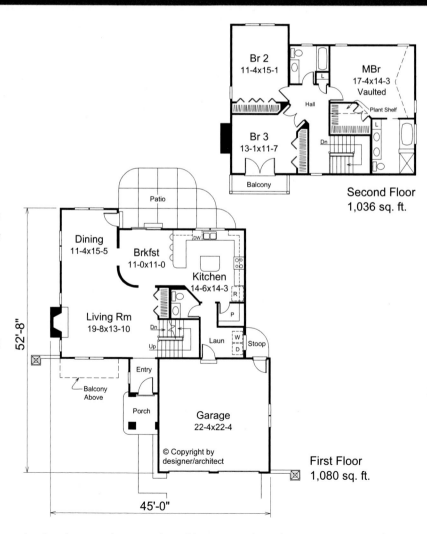

Second Floor
1,036 sq. ft.

First Floor
1,080 sq. ft.

© Copyright by designer/architect

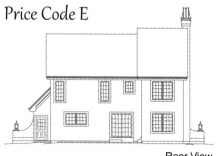

To order this plan, visit the Menards Building Materials Desk or visit www.Menards.com.

Plan #M07-055L-0070

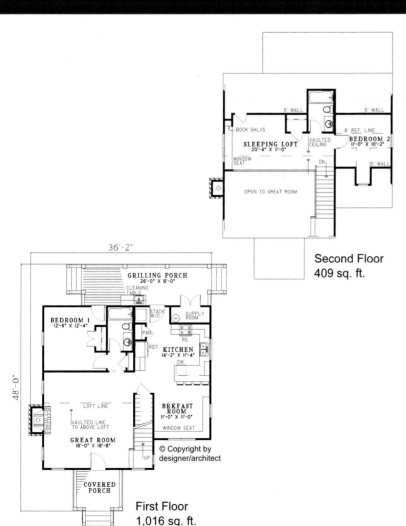

Second Floor
409 sq. ft.

First Floor
1,016 sq. ft.

Unique Cabin With Sleeping Loft

1,425 total square feet of living area

2 bedrooms, 2 baths

Crawl space or slab foundation, please specify when ordering

Special features

The great room features a vaulted ceiling and fireplace

The sleeping loft boasts a vaulted ceiling, window seat and bookshelves

A unique built-in window seat graces the breakfast room

The rear grilling porch includes a cleaning table with built-in sink which is perfect for cleaning game or fish

Price Code A

To order this plan, visit the Menards Building Materials Desk or visit www.Menards.com.

113

Cottage Home Plans

Plan #M07-055L-0067

Comfortable Sports Cabin

1,472 total square feet of living area

3 bedrooms, 2 baths

Crawl space or slab foundation, please specify when ordering

Special features

8' wrap-around porch entry is inviting and creates an outdoor living area

The great room has a rock hearth fireplace and is open to the second floor above

The side grilling porch has a cleaning sink for fish or game

Optional bonus room on the second floor has an additional 199 square feet of living area

Price Code A

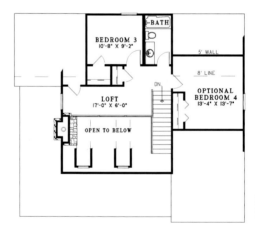

BEDROOM 3
10'-8" X 9'-2"

BATH

5' WALL

8' LINE

LOFT
17'-0" X 6'-0"

DN.

OPTIONAL BEDROOM 4
13'-4" X 13'-7"

OPEN TO BELOW

Second Floor
332 sq. ft.

44'-2"

© Copyright by designer/architect

BATH

GRILLING PORCH
13'-4" X 9'-6"

CLEANING TABLE

BEDROOM 1
11'-0" X 13'-0"

BEDROOM 2
10'-8" X 9'-2"

PAN.

SUPPLY ROOM

STACKED W/D

REF.   RG.

KITCHEN
13'-4" X 12'-6"

DW

GREAT RM.
17'-0" X 16'-0"

UP

39'-0"

8' COVERED PORCH

DINING
13'-4" X 12'-6"

First Floor
1,140 sq. ft.

Plan #M07-007D-0128

52'-0"

40'-8"

Shop

MBr
11-7x15-6

Br 2
10-0x12-11

Garage
21-8x26-4

Hall

Kit
9-7x9-0

Patio

© Copyright by
designer/architect

Living
14-0x18-9

Brk fst
10-9x9-0

Screened Porch
18-4x13-0

E

Porch

First Floor
1,072 sq. ft.

D W

Br 3
13-4x12-3

Basement

Hall

Optional
Lower Level

Basement

Cottage With Screened Porch, Garage And Shop

1,072 total square feet of living area

2 bedrooms, 2 baths

2-car side entry garage

Basement foundation

Special features

Integrated open and screened front porches guarantee comfortable summer enjoyment

The oversized garage includes area for shop and miscellaneous storage

The U-shaped kitchen and breakfast nook are adjacent to the living room and have access to the screened porch

345 square feet of optional living area on the lower level including a third bedroom and a bath

Price Code AA

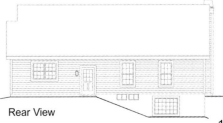

Rear View

To order this plan, visit the Menards Building Materials Desk or visit www.Menards.com.

115

Safe Harbor

MENARDS

Plan #M07-055L-0065

Sportman's Den Cabin

1,397 total square feet of living area

3 bedrooms, 2 baths

Crawl space or slab foundation, please specify when ordering

Special features

A wrap-around 8' porch adds outdoor living area to this design

The den with fireplace has an open view to kitchen with eat-in snack bar

A supply room allows space for hunting gear or tackle storage

Price Code A

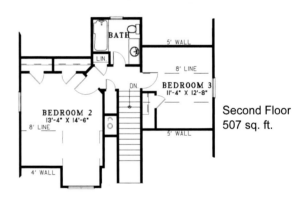

BATH

LIN

BEDROOM 2
13'-4" X 14'-6"

8' LINE

DN.

5' WALL

8' LINE

BEDROOM 3
11'-4" X 12'-8"

5' WALL

4' WALL

Second Floor
507 sq. ft.

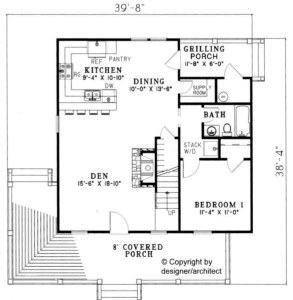

39'-8"

KITCHEN
9'-4" X 10'-10"

REF   PANTRY

RG.

DW.

DINING
10'-0" X 13'-6"

GRILLING
PORCH
11'-8" X 6'-0"

SUPPLY
ROOM

BATH

STACK
W/D

DEN
15'-6" X 18'-10"

UP

BEDROOM 1
11'-4" X 11'-0"

38'-4"

8' COVERED
PORCH

© Copyright by
designer/architect

First Floor
890 sq. ft.

To order this plan, visit the Menards Building Materials Desk or visit www.Menards.com.

Plan #M07-055L-0071

This Cabin Will Provide Fond Memories

1,542 total square feet of living area

2 bedrooms, 2 baths

Crawl space or slab foundation, please specify when ordering

Special features

The den has a vaulted ceiling and walk-around fireplace

The kitchen features an eating bar and island work area

The rear grilling porch with supply room and kitchen access is a convenient feature

Price Code B

Second Floor
383 sq. ft.

First Floor
1,159 sq. ft.

BATH

5' WALL

8' LINE

BEDROOM 2
14'-0" X 18'-0"

DN

BALCONY

VAULTED CEILING

OPEN TO BELOW

37'-2"

45'-0"

BATH

SUPPLY ROOM

GRILLING PORCH
10'-6" X 8'-0"

BEDROOM 1
15'-4" X 14'-0"

LIN

WINDOW SEAT

REF.

RG

STACKED W/D

ISLAND

KITCHEN
14'-0" X 13'-4"

DW

UP

VAULTED CEILING
DEN
20'-10" X 18'-2"

DINING
14'-4" X 12'-0"

© Copyright by designer/architect

COVERED PORCH
21'-6" X 8'-0"

To order this plan, visit the Menards Building Materials Desk or visit www.Menards.com.

117

Fernberry

MENARDS

Cottage Home Plans

Plan #M07-013L-0133

Delightful Country Cabin

953 total square feet of living area

2 bedrooms, 1 1/2 baths

Crawl space foundation

Special features

Relax on porches fit for charming rocking chairs

With two large bedrooms that feature oversized closets, a spacious kitchen and a family room with a fireplace, this home has everything you need to enjoy a vacation getaway

The kitchen has a sunny corner double sink, roomy center island/snack bar and shares a vaulted ceiling with the family room

Price Code A

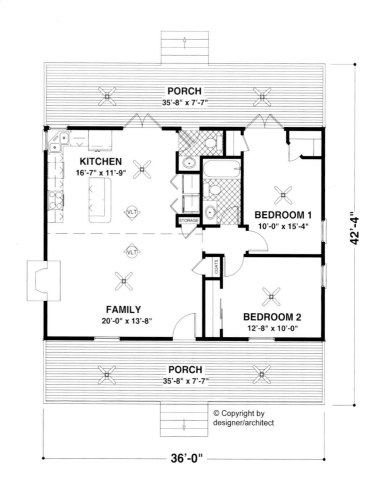

Plan #M07-007D-0199

Ideal Cottage
For Leisure Living

496 total square feet of living area

1 bedroom, 1 bath

2-car garage

Slab foundation

Special features

The traditional front exterior and rear both enjoy shady porches for relaxing evenings

The living room with bayed dining area is open to a functional L-shaped kitchen with a convenient pantry

A full bath, large walk-in closet and access to both the rear porch and the garage enhance the spacious bedroom

Price Code AAA

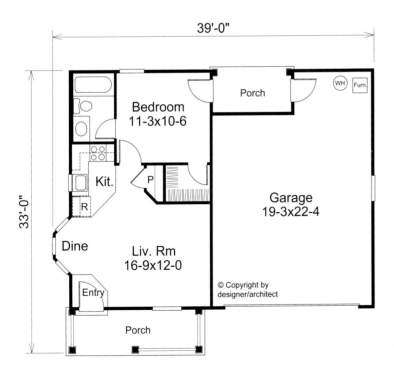

39'-0"

33'-0"

Bedroom
11-3x10-6

Porch

WH Furn.

Kit.

P

R

Garage
19-3x22-4

Dine

Liv. Rm
16-9x12-0

© Copyright by designer/architect

Entry

Porch

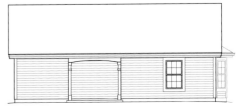

Rear View

To order this plan, visit the Menards Building Materials Desk or visit www.Menards.com.

119

Plan #M07-055L-0101

Relaxed Living In This Ranch

1,903 total square feet of living area

2 bedrooms, 2 baths

2-car garage

Crawl space or slab foundation, please specify when ordering

Special features

A rear screened porch accesses the dining area

The sleeping loft on the second floor has French doors that overlook to great room below

An eat-in counter in the kitchen overlooks the great room

Price Code C

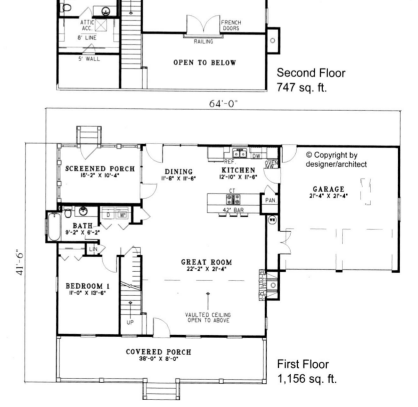

Second Floor
747 sq. ft.

First Floor
1,156 sq. ft.

To order this plan, visit the Menards Building Materials Desk or visit www.Menards.com.

Plan #M07-007D-0109

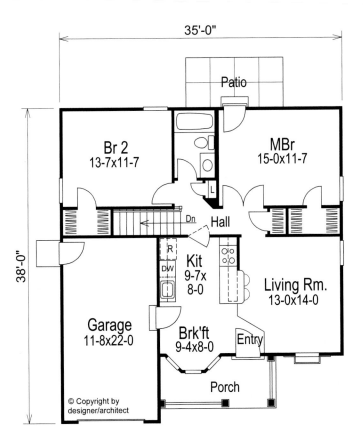

35'-0"

38'-0"

Patio

Br 2
13-7x11-7

MBr
15-0x11-7

Dn Hall

Kit
9-7x
8-0

Living Rm.
13-0x14-0

Garage
11-8x22-0

Brk'ft
9-4x8-0

Entry

Porch

© Copyright by
designer/architect

Elegance In A Starter Or Retirement Home

888 total square feet of living area

2 bedrooms, 1 bath

1-car garage

Basement foundation

Special features

This home features an eye-catching exterior and has a spacious porch

The breakfast room with bay window is open to the living room and adjoins the kitchen with a pass-through snack bar

The roomy bedrooms feature walk-in closets

The master bedroom has a double-door entry and access to the rear patio

Price Code AAA

Rear View

To order this plan, visit the Menards Building Materials Desk or visit www.Menards.com.

121

Cottage Home Plans

Plan #M07-077L-0008

Quaint Cottage

600 total square feet of living area

1 bedroom, 1 bath

Slab, basement, or crawl space foundation, please specify when ordering

Special features

This small home features a spacious living room that connects to the efficient kitchen with a raised snack bar

The kitchen and bedroom access the rear porch and covered or screened porch that offers exceptional outdoor living space

A bonus room is provided for a hobby room or second bedroom and is included in the square footage

Price Code B

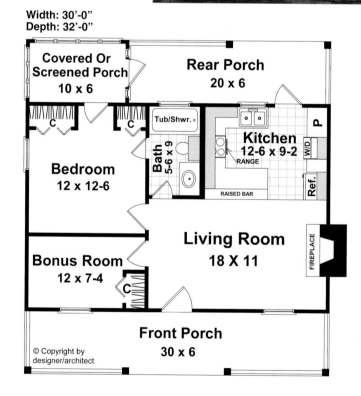

Width: 30'-0"
Depth: 32'-0"

Covered Or Screened Porch 10 x 6

Rear Porch 20 x 6

C   C

Tub/Shwr.

Bath 5-6 x 9

Kitchen 12-6 x 9-2

RANGE

W/D   P

Ref.

Bedroom 12 x 12-6

RAISED BAR

Living Room 18 X 11

FIREPLACE

Bonus Room 12 x 7-4

C

Front Porch 30 x 6

© Copyright by designer/architect

To order this plan, visit the Menards Building Materials Desk or visit www.Menards.com.

Foxton

Plan #M07-055L-0068

Second Floor
304 sq. ft.

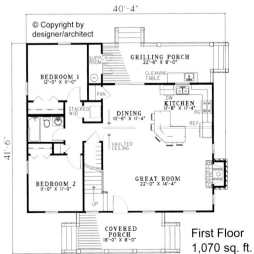

First Floor
1,070 sq. ft.

Two-Story Living Spaces Enlarge This Home

1,374 total square feet of living area

3 bedrooms, 2 baths

Crawl space or slab foundation, please specify when ordering

Special features

The L-shaped counterspace in the kitchen seats five people

The spacious grilling porch is accessible from the dining room for convenience and also features a cleaning and preparation area

There is a versatile bedroom/storage area on the second floor

Price Code A

To order this plan, visit the *Menards* Building Materials Desk or visit www.Menards.com.

123

Cottage Home Plans

Plan #M07-055L-0064

Cabin Cottage With French Door Entry

1,544 total square feet of living area

3 bedrooms, 2 baths

Crawl space or slab foundation, please specify when ordering

Special features

Energy efficient home with 2" x 6" exterior walls

The great room has a vaulted ceiling and fireplace

The 32' x 8' grilling porch in the rear also features a supply room and cleaning table with sink

The kitchen features a center island for great function

Price Code C

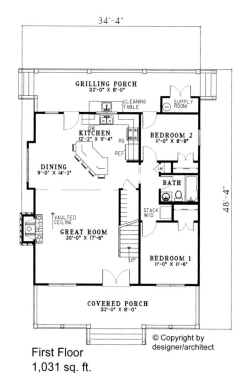

First Floor
1,031 sq. ft.

© Copyright by designer/architect

Second Floor
513 sq. ft.

To order this plan, visit the *Menards* Building Materials Desk or visit *www.Menards.com*.

Plan #M07-007D-0133

Porches Enhance Small Retirement Or Starter Home

1,316 total square feet of living area

2 bedrooms, 2 baths

2-car side entry garage

Basement foundation, drawings also include crawl space and slab foundations

Special features

Porches are accessible from the entry, dining room and study/bedroom #2

The living room enjoys a vaulted ceiling, corner fireplace and twin transomed windows

The kitchen has corner windows, an outdoor plant shelf, a snack bar, a built-in pantry and opens to a large dining room

Roomy bedrooms feature walk-in closets and have easy access to oversized baths

Price Code A

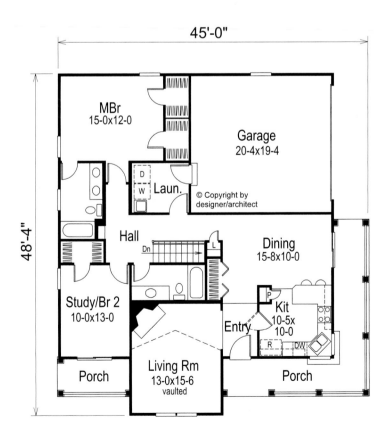

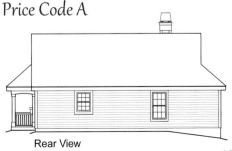

Rear View

To order this plan, visit the Menards Building Materials Desk or visit www.Menards.com.

125

Plan #M07-024L-0011

Double Dormers
Add Curb Appeal

1,819 total square feet of living area

3 bedrooms, 2 1/2 baths

Crawl space or slab foundation, please specify when ordering

Special features

Unique bath layout on the second floor allows for both bedrooms to have their own private sink area while connecting to a central bath

The window wall in the dining area floods the space with sunlight

Walk-in closets can be found in every bedroom

Price Code C

Width: 38'-0"
Depth: 42'-0"

Deck

Breakfast
10'10"x 16'

Kitchen
14'6"x 10'2"

Dining
13'x 12'

Utility

Bath

1/2 Bath

WIC

Living
13'x 20'

Bedroom
12'x 15'

© Copyright by designer/architect

Porch

First Floor
1,242 sq. ft.

WIC

Bath

WIC

Bedroom
13'x 11'

Bedroom
12'x 11'

Open to Below

Second Floor
577 sq. ft.

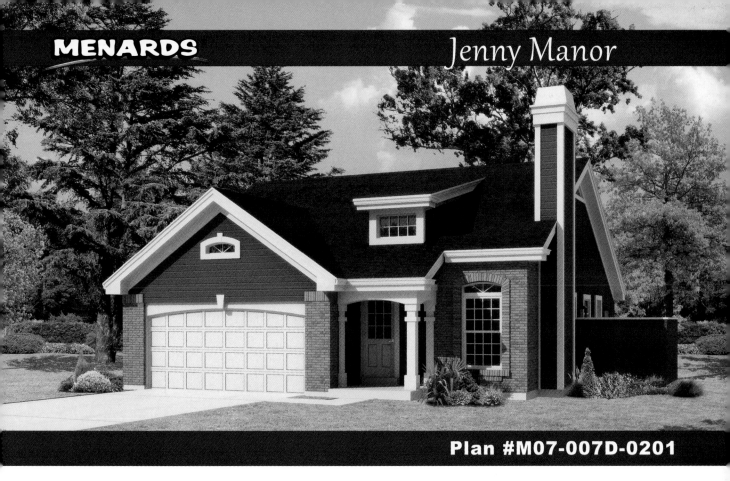

Plan #M07-007D-0201

Functional Design
For Compact Lot

1,153 total square feet of living area

3 bedrooms, 2 baths

2-car garage

Basement foundation

Special features

The arched window, detailed brickwork and roof dormer all combine to create a stylish and inviting exterior

A fireplace, U-shaped kitchen with built-in pantry and dining area with view to a side fenced patio are the many features of the living room

The master bedroom includes a private bath, walk-in closet and access to the patio

Price Code A

37'-4"

47'-8"

Br 2
11-0x11-0

MBr
12-3x13-0

Br 3
11-0x9-0

Hall

Kitchen
12-3x9-2

DW

Patio

DN

L

Dine

Living Room
14-8x17-10

Garage
19-4x20-4

© Copyright by designer/architect

Entry

Porch

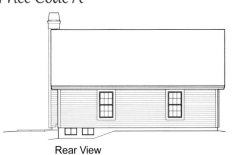

Rear View

To order this plan, visit the Menards Building Materials Desk or visit www.Menards.com.

127

Oakford

Plan #M07-007D-0173

Inviting Spacious Home

2,121 total square feet of living area

4 bedrooms, 3 1/2 baths

2-car garage

Basement foundation, drawings also include slab and crawl space foundations

Special features

The spacious great room includes a corner fireplace, dining area with bay window and glass sliding doors to the rear patio

A huge center island with seating for six, built-in pantry and 26' of counterspace are just a few amenities of the awesome kitchen

Three generously sized bedrooms with two baths comprise the second floor

Price Code C

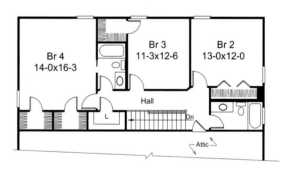

Br 4
14-0x16-3

Br 3
11-3x12-6

Br 2
13-0x12-0

Hall

Attic

Second Floor
915 sq. ft.

47'-0"

Patio

Living Rm.
19-3x19-8

MBr
16-0x12-6

Dining

Hall

Laun.

Kit
14-4x13-7

Up

Dn

Entry

Porch

Garage
20-4x21-4

42'-0"

© Copyright by
designer/architect

First Floor
1,206 sq. ft.

Rear View

To order this plan, visit the Menards Building Materials Desk or visit www.Menards.com.

Plan #M07-013L-0129

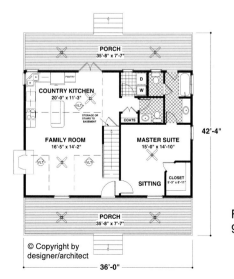

Second Floor
381 sq. ft.

BEDROOM 3
13'-2" x 10'-0"

6' HIGH KNEE WALL

OPEN BELOW
16'-5" x 23'-0"

BEDROOM 2
15'-0" x 12'-8"

6' HIGH KNEE WALL

PORCH
35'-8" x 7'-7"

COUNTRY KITCHEN
20'-0" x 11'-3"

PANTRY

D W

STORAGE OR STAIRS TO BASEMENT

COATS

FAMILY ROOM
16'-5" x 14'-2"

MASTER SUITE
15'-0" x 14'-10"

SITTING

CLOSET
5'-3" x 6'-11"

PORCH
35'-8" x 7'-7"

42'-4"

First Floor
953 sq. ft.

36'-0"

© Copyright by designer/architect

Open Floor Plan

1,334 total square feet of living area

3 bedrooms, 2 1/2 baths

Crawl space foundation

Special features

This welcoming design is ideal for a vacation, starter or empty-nester home

Relax on the cozy front and rear porches that are large enough for rocking chairs

The spacious first floor master suite features a walk-in closet, sitting area and private bath

The second floor features two bedrooms that share a full bath

Price Code D

To order this plan, visit the Menards Building Materials Desk or visit www.Menards.com.

129

Simmons

Plan #M07-077L-0178

Charming Curb Appeal

1,900 total square feet of living area

3 bedrooms, 2 1/2 baths

2-car side entry garage

Slab or crawl space foundation, please specify when ordering

Special features

The breakfast area enjoys the view of the large fireplace located in the great room

The master bedroom is separated from the other bedrooms for privacy and features a luxury bath and two walk-in closets

The dining/office is a versatile space that can adapt to your needs

The bonus room above the garage has an additional 348 square feet of living area

Price Code D

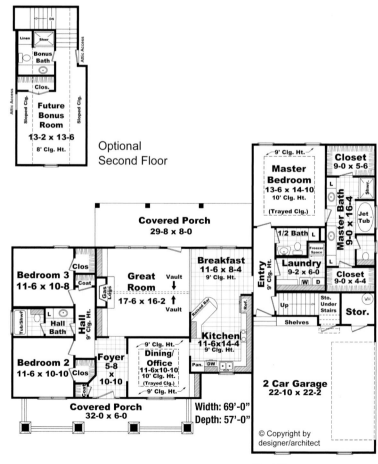

Optional Second Floor

First Floor
1,900 sq. ft.

Plan #M07-008D-0140

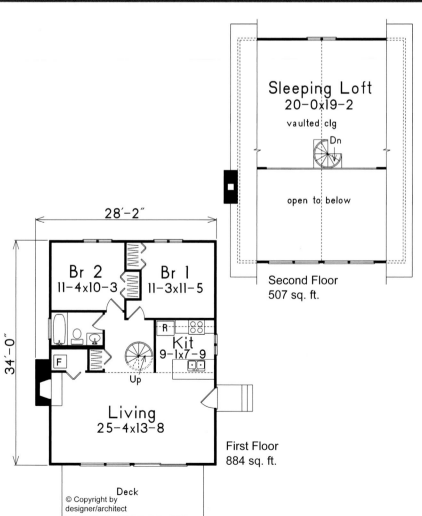

Sleeping Loft
20–0x19–2
vaulted clg

Dn

open to below

Second Floor
507 sq. ft.

28'–2"

Br 2
11–4x10–3

Br 1
11–3x11–5

34'–0"

R

Kit
9–1x7–9

F

Up

Living
25–4x13–8

First Floor
884 sq. ft.

Deck

© Copyright by
designer/architect

Cozy Vacation Retreat

1,391 total square feet of living area

2 bedrooms, 1 bath

Pier foundation, drawings also
include crawl space foundation

Special features

The large living room with masonry fireplace
features a soaring vaulted ceiling

A spiral staircase in the hall leads to a
huge sleeping loft overlooking the living
room below

Two first floor bedrooms share a full bath

Price Code A

To order this plan, visit the Menards Building Materials Desk or visit www.Menards.com.

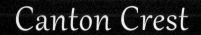

MENARDS

Plan #M07-013L-0154

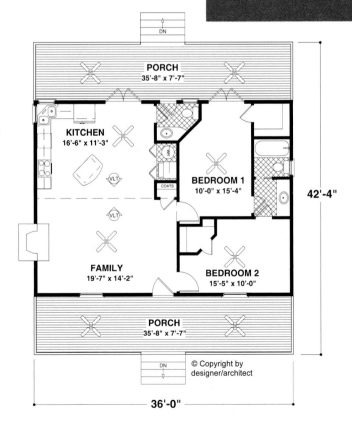

Great Porch Opportunities

953 total square feet of living area

2 bedrooms, 1 1/2 baths

Crawl space foundation

Special features

Covered front and rear porches feature ceiling fans to keep you comfortable in warmer weather

Two generous bedrooms, each with a walk-in closet, share a spacious bathroom

A dramatic vaulted ceiling crowns the open family room and kitchen

Price Code A

To order this plan, visit the Menards Building Materials Desk or visit www.Menards.com.

Plan #M07-007D-0181

Charming
Three-Bedroom Home

1,140 total square feet of living area

3 bedrooms, 2 baths

2-car garage

Basement foundation, drawings also include slab and crawl space foundations

Special features

Delightful appearance with a protective porch

The entry, with convenient stairs to the basement, leads to spacious living and dining rooms open to the adjacent kitchen

The master bedroom enjoys a double-door entry, walk-in closet and a private bath with its own linen closet

Price Code AA

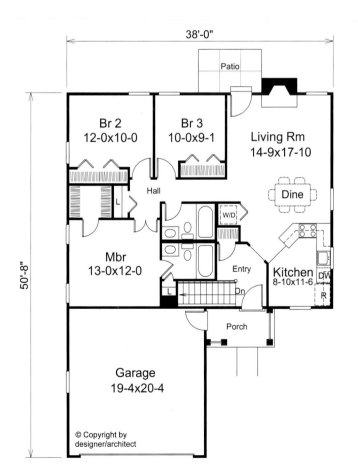

Br 2
12-0x10-0

Br 3
10-0x9-1

Living Rm
14-9x17-10

Hall

Dine

Mbr
13-0x12-0

W/D

Entry

Kitchen
8-10x11-6

DW

Dn

Porch

Garage
19-4x20-4

38'-0"

50'-8"

Patio

© Copyright by designer/architect

Rear View

To order this plan, visit the Menards Building Materials Desk or visit www.Menards.com.

133

Parham

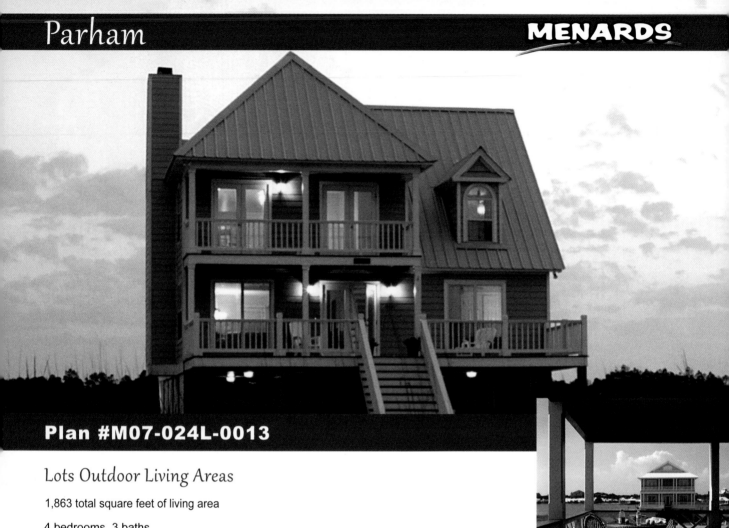

Plan #M07-024L-0013

Lots Outdoor Living Areas

1,863 total square feet of living area

4 bedrooms, 3 baths

Pier foundation

Special features

The luxurious master bedroom has a private bath, double walk-in closets and two sets of double French doors leading onto the balcony

The kitchen is open to the dining area and includes a center island large enough for eating

The bedrooms on the second floor both enjoy a private bath and lots of closet space

Price Code C

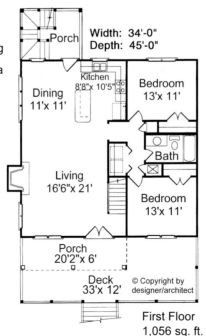

Porch

Width: 34'-0"
Depth: 45'-0"

Kitchen
8'8" x 10'5"

Dining
11' x 11'

Bedroom
13' x 11'

Living
16'6" x 21'

Bath

Bedroom
13' x 11'

Porch
20'2" x 6'

Deck
33' x 12'

© Copyright by designer/architect

First Floor
1,056 sq. ft.

Ma. Bath

Bath

Master Bedroom
16'6" x 19'

Bedroom
13' x 13'

Balcony
20'2" x 6'

Second Floor
807 sq. ft.

To order this plan, visit the Menards Building Materials Desk or visit www.Menards.com.

Plan #M07-055L-0508

Second Floor
896 sq. ft.

First Floor
998 sq. ft.

This Country Style Home Has A High-Pitched Roof

1,894 total square feet of living area

3 bedrooms, 2 1/2 baths

2-car garage

Crawl space or slab foundation, please specify when ordering

Special features

The center fireplace warms the entire great room that spans the entire depth of this home

The second floor master suite is topped with a tray ceiling and has an amenity-filled private bath

The extended counter in the kitchen features enough casual dining space for four people

The bonus room on the second floor has an additional 300 square feet of living area

Price Code C

To order this plan, visit the *Menards* Building Materials Desk or visit www.Menards.com.

135

Plan #M07-121D-0017

Handsome Two Bedroom Ranch

1,379 total square feet of living area

2 bedrooms, 1 bath

2-car garage

Basement foundation

Special features

The kitchen shares the center island and eating bar with the open great room for easy meals

Both bedrooms have ample closet space and enjoy bay windows

The vaulted breakfast area boasts a bay window with access to the rear patio

Price Code AA

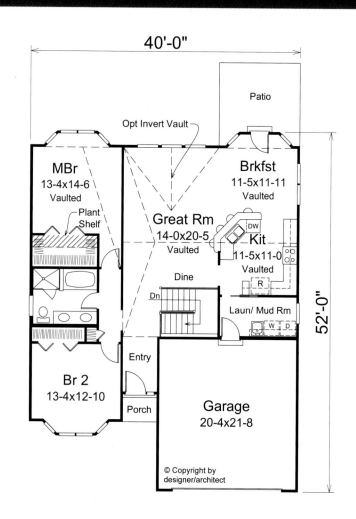

Rear View

To order this plan, visit the Menards Building Materials Desk or visit www.Menards.com.

Plan #M07-007D-0112

Excellent Home For A Small Family

1,062 total square feet of living area

3 bedrooms, 2 baths

2-car garage

Basement foundation

Special features

Handsome appeal is created by the triple-gable facade

The efficient U-shaped kitchen features a snack bar, breakfast area and is open to the living room with a bay window

Both the master bedroom, with its own private bath, and bedroom #2/study enjoy access to the rear patio

Price Code AA

42'-8"

45'-0"

Patio

Br 3
10-0x11-5

Br 2 /
Study
9-5x9-2

MBr
12-0x11-5

Hall

Dn

Kit
8-4x,
8-4

DW

Living Rm.
12-10x14-0

Brk'ft
9-6x8-9

Garage
19-4x20-4

Entry

Porch

© Copyright by designer/architect

Rear View

To order this plan, visit the Menards Building Materials Desk or visit www.Menards.com.

137

Towercliff

Plan #M07-001D-0119

Layout Creates Large Open Living Area

1,285 total square feet of living area

3 bedrooms, 2 baths

Crawl space foundation, drawings also include basement and slab foundations

Special features

Energy efficient home with 2" x 6" exterior walls

Accommodating home with a ranch style front porch and large storage area in the back

The master bedroom includes a dressing area, private bath and built-in bookcase

The kitchen features a pantry, breakfast bar and open view to the dining room

Price Code B

48'-0"

37'-8"

Storage

D
W

Kit
9-10x
10-11

R

Dining
10-3x
10-11

MBr
12-0x14-5

Furn L

P

Living
18-10x14-2

Br 2
15-6x10-8

Br 3
10-1x10-8

© Copyright by designer/architect

Porch depth 6-0

Rear View

To order this plan, visit the *Menards Building Materials Desk* or visit *www.Menards.com*.

Plan #M07-024L-0006

Loaded With Charm

1,618 total square feet of living area

3 bedrooms, 2 1/2 baths

Slab or pier foundation, please specify when ordering

Special features

The secondary bedrooms include walk-in closets and share the second floor bath

The utility room is tucked away in the kitchen for convenience, but is out of sight

The dining area is brightened by a large bay window

Price Code C

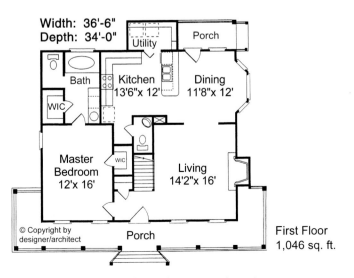

Second Floor
572 sq. ft.

First Floor
1,046 sq. ft.

© Copyright by designer/architect

To order this plan, visit the Menards Building Materials Desk or visit www.Menards.com.

139

Marina Bay

Plan #M07-007D-0244

Atrium Home With Sunbelt Style

1,605 total square feet of living area

2 bedrooms, 2 baths

2-car side entry garage

Walk-out basement foundation

Special features

A stucco exterior, wrap-around columned porch and palladian windows with custom grilles are a few of this home's unique design features

The great room offers a bay window, fireplace, access to the rear deck and a dining balcony

The two-story atrium is 168 square feet and is included in the total square footage

The U-shaped kitchen has a snack bar and a convenient adjacent laundry room

Double-entry doors lead you into the master bedroom that enjoys an awesome luxury bath and walk-in closet

Price Code C

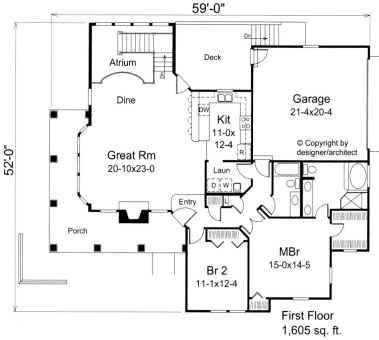

First Floor
1,605 sq. ft.

Lower Level

Unfinished Basement

Rear View

140

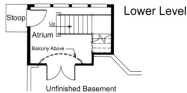

Plan #M07-022D-0009

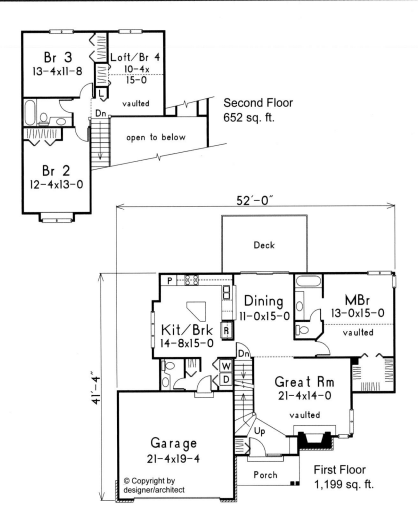

Second Floor 652 sq. ft.

Br 3
13-4x11-8

Loft/Br 4
10-4x
15-0
vaulted

Br 2
12-4x13-0

open to below

First Floor 1,199 sq. ft.

52'-0"

41'-4"

Deck

Kit/Brk
14-8x15-0

Dining
11-0x15-0

MBr
13-0x15-0
vaulted

Great Rm
21-4x14-0
vaulted

Garage
21-4x19-4

Porch

© Copyright by designer/architect

Vaulted Great Room With Open Entrance

1,851 total square feet of living area

4 bedrooms, 2 1/2 baths

2-car garage

Basement foundation

Special features

The high-impact entrance to the great room also leads directly to the second floor

The first floor master bedroom suite features a corner window and walk-in closet

The kitchen/breakfast room has a center work island and pass-through to the dining room

Second floor bedrooms share a bath

Price Code D

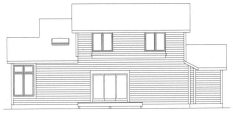

Rear View

To order this plan, visit the Menards Building Materials Desk or visit www.Menards.com.

141

Plan #M07-008D-0078

Wonderful Victorian Styling

1,971 total square feet of living area

3 bedrooms, 2 1/2 baths

2-car garage

Basement foundation

Special features

The great room, kitchen and breakfast area unite to provide a central living space

The unique parlor offers a place for nice conversation off the dining area

The deluxe master bedroom has a walk-in closet and sunny master bath

Price Code C

First Floor
1,032 sq. ft.

Second Floor
939 sq. ft.

© Copyright by designer/architect

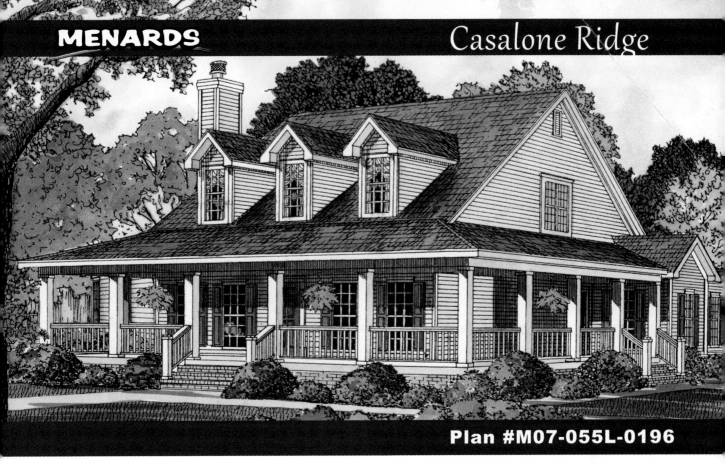

Plan #M07-055L-0196

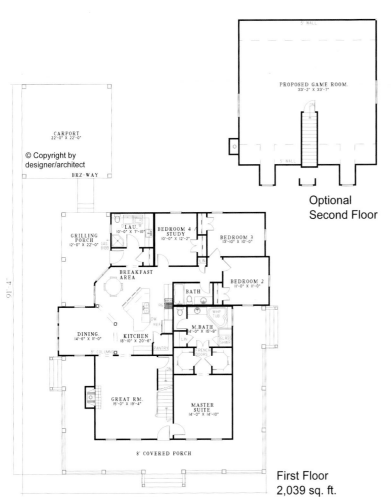

CARPORT
22'-0" X 22'-0"

© Copyright by designer/architect

BRZ-WAY

PROPOSED GAME ROOM
33'-2" X 33'-7"

Optional
Second Floor

GRILLING PORCH
12'-0" X 22'-0"

LAU. W

BEDROOM 4 STUDY
10'-0" X 7'-10"

BEDROOM 3
13'-10" X 12'-2"

BREAKFAST AREA

BEDROOM 2
11'-0" X 11'-0"

BATH

DINING
14'-6" X 11'-0"

KITCHEN
18'-10" X 20'-6"

M. BATH
14'-0" X 15'-8"

PANTRY

WHP TUB

GLASS SHWR

8' COLUMN

FRENCH DOORS

GREAT RM.
15'-0" X 19'-4"

MASTER SUITE
14'-0" X 14'-10"

8' COVERED PORCH

First Floor
2,039 sq. ft.

60'-6"

Rear Grilling Porch

2,039 total square feet of living area

4 bedrooms, 3 baths

2-car detached carport

Slab or crawl space foundation, please specify when ordering

Special features

A walk-in pantry and extra-large island add convenience to the open kitchen

Columns define the formal dining room

The luxurious master suite features two walk-in closets and French doors leading to the relaxing master bath

The optional second floor has an additional 1,155 square feet of living space

Price Code D

To order this plan, visit the *Menards* Building Materials Desk or visit www.Menards.com.

143

Plan #M07-058D-0014

Year-Round Hideaway

416 total square feet of living area

Sleeping area, 1 bath

Slab foundation

Special features

The open floor plan of this home creates a spacious feeling

The covered porch has rustic appeal

The kitchen offers plenty of cabinets and workspace

A large linen closet is centrally located and close to the bath

2" x 6" exterior walls available, please order plan #M07-058D-0076

Price Code AAA

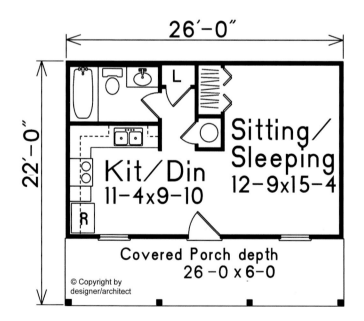

26'-0"

22'-0"

Kit/Din
11-4x9-10

Sitting/
Sleeping
12-9x15-4

L

Covered Porch depth
26-0 x 6-0

© Copyright by designer/architect

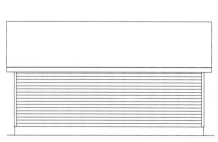

Rear View

Plan #M07-007D-0237

Striking Two-Story Home

1,994 total square feet of living area

3 bedrooms, 2 1/2 baths

2-car garage

Basement, crawl space or slab foundation, please specify when ordering

Special features

A double sink with corner windows, snack bar island, walk-in pantry and a bayed breakfast area are the features of the kitchen

The vaulted master bedroom has a luxury bath with linen closet

The large great room enjoys a fireplace with flanking windows

Price Code B

First Floor
1,002 sq. ft.

Patio

Brkfst 9-0x12-0

Dining 12-0x12-0

Kitchen 13-6x17-7

Great Rm 17-5x19-6

R

P

W D

Laun

E

Porch

Garage 19-4x21-4

© Copyright by designer/architect

53'-8"

34'-0"

MBr 13-7x16-9 Vaulted

Br 2 10-6x13-0

Hall

Br 3 10-6x13-0

L

Second Floor
992 sq. ft.

Rear View

To order this plan, visit the Menards Building Materials Desk or visit www.Menards.com.

145

Plan #M07-014D-0009

Vaulted Ceilings Throughout Create Dramatic Interior

1,428 total square feet of living area

3 bedrooms, 2 baths

2-car garage

Basement foundation, drawings also include crawl space foundation

Special features

Energy efficient home with 2" x 6" exterior walls

10' ceilings in the entry and hallway

Vaulted secondary bedrooms

The kitchen is loaded with amenities including an island with a salad sink and pantry

The vaulted master bedroom includes a large walk-in closet and private master bath

Price Code A

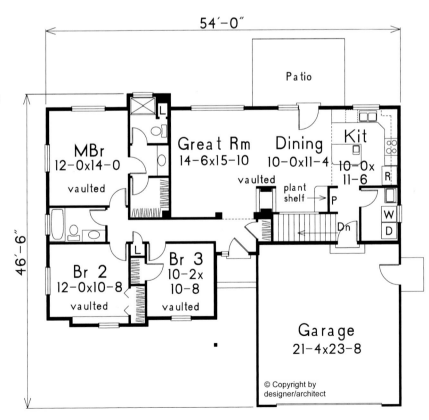

Rear View

To order this plan, visit the Menards Building Materials Desk or visit www.Menards.com.

Plan #M07-001D-0031

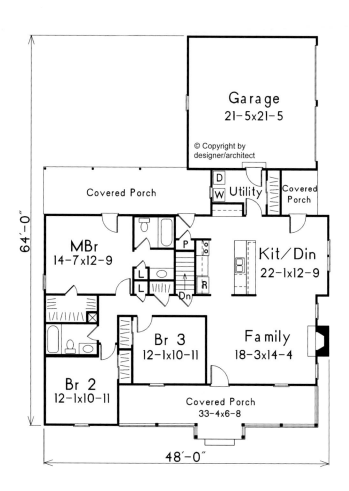

Country-Style Home With Large Front Porch

1,501 total square feet of living area

3 bedrooms, 2 baths

2-car side entry garage

Basement foundation, drawings also include crawl space and slab foundations

Special features

The spacious kitchen/dining area is open to the covered porch

A convenient utility room is adjacent to the garage

The master bedroom features a private bath, dressing area and access to the large covered porch

The large family room creates openness

Price Code B

Rear View

Edison

Plan #M07-057D-0012

Perfect Design For A Narrow Lot

1,112 total square feet of living area

3 bedrooms, 1 bath

Basement foundation

Special features

Energy efficient home with 2" x 6" exterior walls

Brick, an arched window and a planter box decorate the facade of this lovely ranch home

The eat-in kitchen offers an abundance of counterspace and enjoys access to the outdoors

Three bedrooms are situated together for easy family living

Price Code AA

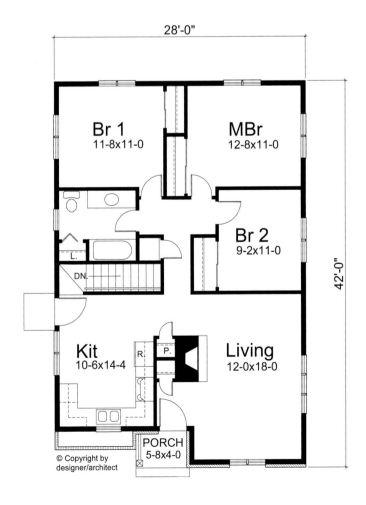

28'-0"

42'-0"

Br 1
11-8x11-0

MBr
12-8x11-0

Br 2
9-2x11-0

DN.

L.

Kit
10-6x14-4

R. P.

Living
12-0x18-0

PORCH
5-8x4-0

© Copyright by
designer/architect

To order this plan, visit the Menards Building Materials Desk or visit www.Menards.com.

Plan #M07-121D-0007

24'-0"

Detached Garage
23-4x23-4

24'-0"

© Copyright by
designer/architect

Spacious Great Room

1,308 total square feet of living area

3 bedrooms, 2 baths

2-car detached garage

Basement foundation

Special features

A lovely bay window and access to the rear patio are some of the features of the vaulted kitchen/dining area

A tall ceiling and warming fireplace in the great room appeal to every homeowner

The vaulted master bedroom showcases a large walk-in closet, bay window and private bath

Price Code AA

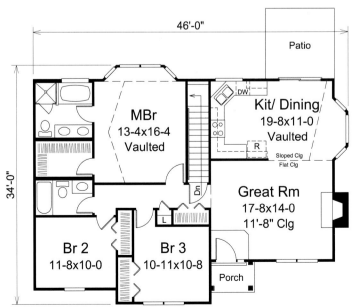

46'-0"

Patio

34'-0"

MBr
13-4x16-4
Vaulted

Kit/ Dining
19-8x11-0
Vaulted

DW

R

Sloped Clg
Flat Clg

Dn

Great Rm
17-8x14-0
11'-8" Clg

L

Br 2
11-8x10-0

Br 3
10-11x10-8

Porch

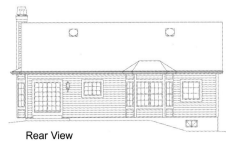

Rear View

Plan #M07-040D-0015

Covered Porch Adds Charm To Entrance

1,655 total square feet of living area

3 bedrooms, 2 baths

2-car garage

Crawl space foundation

Special features

The master bedroom features a 9' ceiling, walk-in closet and bath with a dressing area

The oversized family room includes a 10' ceiling and a masonry see-through fireplace

The island kitchen has convenient access to the laundry room

The handy covered walkway from the garage leads to the kitchen and dining area

Price Code B

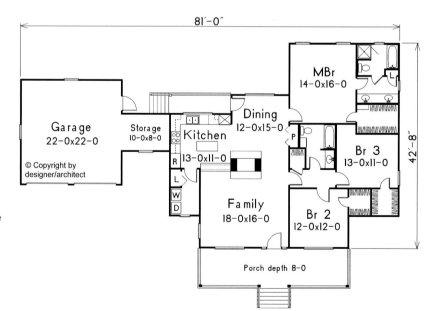

81'-0"

42'-8"

MBr
14-0x16-0

Dining
12-0x15-0

Garage
22-0x22-0

Storage
10-0x8-0

Kitchen
13-0x11-0

Br 3
13-0x11-0

© Copyright by
designer/architect

Family
18-0x16-0

Br 2
12-0x12-0

Porch depth 8-0

Rear View

To order this plan, visit the *Menards* Building Materials Desk or visit www.Menards.com.

Plan #M07-001D-0042

Open Living Space Creates Comfortable Atmosphere

1,000 total square feet of living area

3 bedrooms, 1 bath

Crawl space foundation, drawings also include basement and slab foundations

Special features

Bath includes convenient hide-away laundry area

Master bedroom includes double closets and private access to bath

Foyer features handy coat closet

Kitchen features L-shaped design and easy access outdoors

Price Code AA

40'-0"

25'-0"

MBr
11-8x11-8

Kit/Dining
16-7x11-8

W
D

Furn   R

Br 2
11-8x9-0

Br 3
10-4x9-0

Living
14-5x12-5

Porch

© Copyright by designer/architect

To order this plan, visit the Menards Building Materials Desk or visit www.Menards.com.

151

MENARDS

Plan #M07-045D-0012

Open Layout Ensures Easy Living

976 total square feet of living area

3 bedrooms, 1 1/2 baths

Basement foundation

Special features

The cozy front porch opens into the large living area

All the bedrooms in this home are located on the second floor for privacy

The dining room has access to the outdoors

Price Code AA

Rear View

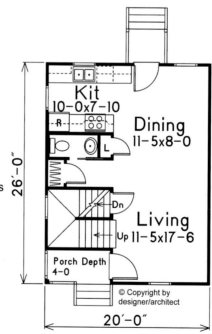

Kit
10-0x7-10

Dining
11-5x8-0

Living
Up 11-5x17-6

Dn

Porch Depth
4-0

26'-0"

20'-0"

© Copyright by designer/architect

First Floor
488 sq. ft.

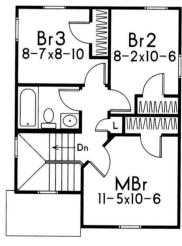

Br3
8-7x8-10

Br2
8-2x10-6

MBr
11-5x10-6

Dn

Second Floor
488 sq. ft.

To order this plan, visit the Menards Building Materials Desk or visit www.Menards.com.

Plan #M07-013L-0014

A Rustic Drive Under Ranch

1,728 total square feet of living area

3 bedrooms, 2 baths

3-car drive under side entry garage

Basement or crawl space foundation, please specify when ordering

Special features

The large entry leads to the family room featuring a corner fireplace and a window wall overlooking an enormous deck

The master bedroom is adorned with a dramatic bath featuring an angled entry and a corner tub

A built-on eating bar extends off the kitchen counter and overlooks the nearby family room

Price Code C

SCREENED PORCH
12'3" x 11'7"

DECK
40'11" x 11'7"

DINING
12'0" x 10'1"

KITCHEN
12'0" x 7'0"

MASTER BDRM
16'0" x 19'8"

FAMILY ROOM
19'0" x 19'8"

PANTRY

DN

BEDRM 3
12'0" x 11'0"

ENTRY

BEDRM 2
12'0" x 11'0"

32'-0"

© Copyright by designer/architect

PORCH
28'4" x 7'7"

◄ 54'-0" ►

To order this plan, visit the Menards Building Materials Desk or visit www.Menards.com.

153

Cornwall

Plan #M07-008D-0088

Embracing The Sun With Skylights

1,850 total square feet of living area

3 bedrooms, 2 1/2 baths

2-car garage

Basement foundation

Special features

The large living room with fireplace is illuminated by three second story skylights

The living and dining rooms are separated by a low wall while the dining room and kitchen are separated by a snack bar creating a spacious atmosphere

The master bedroom has a huge bath with double-bowl vanity and large walk-in closet

Two second floor bedrooms share a uniquely designed bath

Price Code C

Second Floor
630 sq. ft.

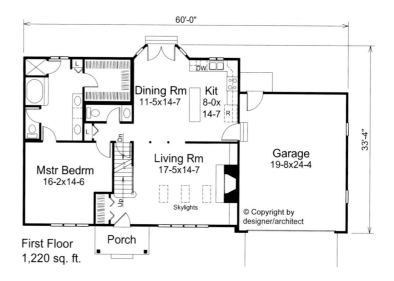

First Floor
1,220 sq. ft.

To order this plan, visit the *Menards* Building Materials Desk or visit www.Menards.com.

Plan #M07-058D-0094

Vaulted Great Room

1,895 total square feet of living area

3 bedrooms, 2 baths

2-car garage

Basement foundation

Special features

Energy efficient home with 2" x 6" exterior walls

The foyer opens into the airy great room that features a grand fireplace

The kitchen/breakfast area enjoys a work island, built-in desk, walk-in pantry and access to the outdoors

Both baths include a double-bowl vanity for convenience

Price Code B

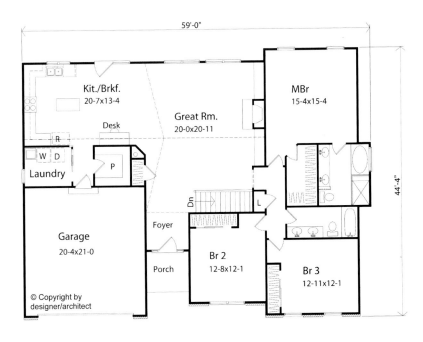

59'-0"

44'-4"

Kit./Brkf.
20-7x13-4

Great Rm.
20-0x20-11

MBr
15-4x15-4

Desk

R

W D

Laundry

P

Garage
20-4x21-0

Foyer

Dn

L

Porch

Br 2
12-8x12-1

Br 3
12-11x12-1

© Copyright by
designer/architect

Brightmoore

Plan #M07-001D-0024

Functional Layout For Comfortable Living

1,360 total square feet of living area

3 bedrooms, 2 baths

2-car side entry garage

Basement foundation, drawings also include crawl space and slab foundations

Special features

The kitchen/dining room features an island workspace and plenty of dining area

The master bedroom has a large walk-in closet and private bath

The laundry room is adjacent to the kitchen for easy access

There is a convenient workshop located in the in garage

The large closets in the secondary bedrooms maintain organization

Price Code A

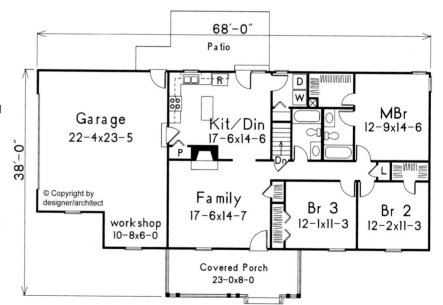

Garage
22-4x23-5

Kit/Din
17-6x14-6

MBr
12-9x14-6

© Copyright by designer/architect

Family
17-6x14-7

Br 3
12-1x11-3

Br 2
12-2x11-3

workshop
10-8x6-0

Covered Porch
23-0x8-0

68'-0"

Patio

38'-0"

Rear View

To order this plan, visit the Menards Building Materials Desk or visit www.Menards.com.

Forest Ridge

Plan #M07-007D-0210

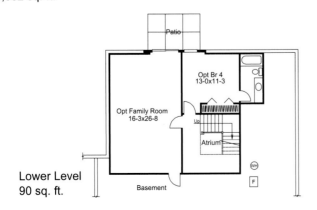

70'-4"

47'-0"

Study/Br 3
11-5x11-5
vaulted

Br 2
11-4x11-5
vaulted

Patio

Patio
Bar

R

Sauna

Covered
Patio
vaulted

skylights
above

Kitchen
13-2x13-2

Hall

R

DW

Atrium
vaulted

MBr
12-10x16-0
vaulted

Garage
21-4x23-0

© Copyright by
designer/architect

Laun
W
D

Dining
16-4x12-10
vaulted

Foyer
vaulted

Living
16-0x13-0
vaulted

Porch

First Floor
1,852 sq. ft.

Patio

Opt Br 4
13-0x11-3

Opt Family Room
16-3x26-8

Up

Atrium

Basement

WH

F

Lower Level
90 sq. ft.

Clerestory Windows
Brighten Atrium Stair

1,942 total square feet of living area

3 bedrooms, 2 1/2 baths

2-car garage

Walk-out basement foundation

Special features

The handsome country contemporary ranch has the look of a two-story

An elongated porch and classy foyer leads into a central atrium with a winding staircase to the lower level

The kitchen is open to the dining area and has views of the covered patio

The lower level features an additional 708 square feet with an optional spacious family room and fourth bedroom with bath

Price Code B

Rear View

To order this plan, visit the Menards Building Materials Desk or visit www.Menards.com.

157

Plan #M07-022D-0002

Floor-To-Ceiling Window Expands Compact Two-Story

1,246 total square feet of living area

3 bedrooms, 2 baths

2-car garage

Basement foundation

Special features

The corner living room window adds openness

The out-of-the-way kitchen with dining area accesses the outdoors

The private first floor master bedroom has interesting corner windows

A large walk-in closet is located in bedroom #3

The easily built perimeter allows for economical construction

Price Code A

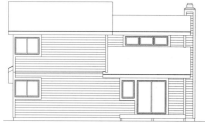

Rear View

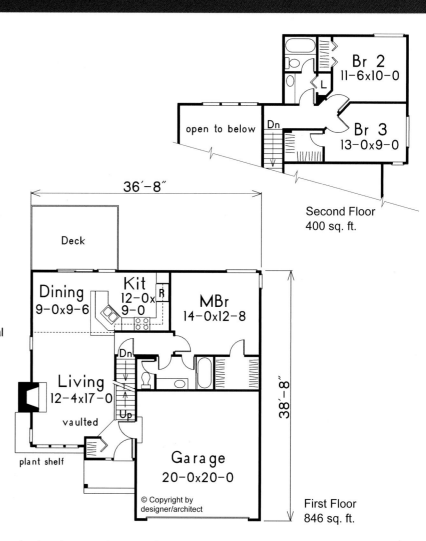

Br 2
11-6x10-0

open to below

Br 3
13-0x9-0

Second Floor
400 sq. ft.

36'-8"

Deck

Dining
9-0x9-6

Kit
12-0x
9-0

MBr
14-0x12-8

Dn

Living
12-4x17-0

vaulted

Up

plant shelf

Garage
20-0x20-0

38'-8"

© Copyright by designer/architect

First Floor
846 sq. ft.

To order this plan, visit the Menards Building Materials Desk or visit www.Menards.com.

Plan #M07-001D-0040

Perfect Home
For A Small Family

864 total square feet of living area

2 bedrooms, 1 bath

Crawl space foundation, drawings also include basement and slab foundations

Special features

An L-shaped kitchen with convenient pantry is adjacent to the dining area

This home has easy access to the laundry, linen and storage closets

Both of the bedrooms in this home include ample closet space

Price Code AAA

36'-0"

28'-0"

Br 1
13-2x10-1

Kit
10-2x6-8

R

D W Furn

Dining
9-5x
10-4

Br 2
11-8x13-0

L L

Living
13-5x13-0

© Copyright by designer/architect

Porch depth 4-0

Rear View

To order this plan, visit the *Menards* Building Materials Desk or visit www.Menards.com.

159

Plan #M07-008D-0147

Unique, Yet Functional Design

1,316 total square feet of living area

3 bedrooms, 1 bath

Crawl space foundation

Special features

The massive vaulted family/living room is accented with a fireplace and views to the outdoors through sliding glass doors

The galley-style kitchen is centrally located

The unique separate shower room near the bath doubles as a convenient mud room

Price Code A

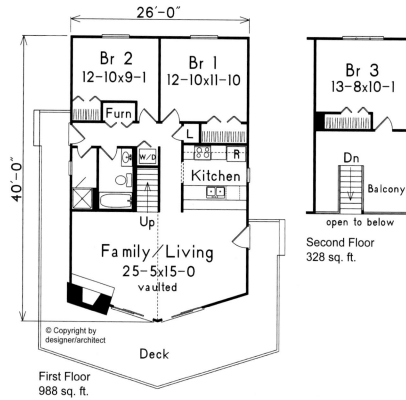

26'-0"

Br 2
12-10x9-1

Br 1
12-10x11-10

Furn

W/D

Kitchen

Up

Family/Living
25-5x15-0
vaulted

© Copyright by
designer/architect

40'-0"

Deck

First Floor
988 sq. ft.

Br 3
13-8x10-1

Dn

Balcony

open to below

Second Floor
328 sq. ft.

To order this plan, visit the *Menards Building Materials Desk* or visit www.Menards.com.

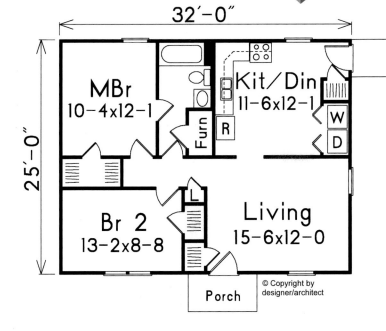

Plan #M07-001D-0088

Ideal For A Starter Home

800 total square feet of living area

2 bedrooms, 1 bath

Crawl space foundation, drawings also include basement foundation

Special features

The master bedroom has a walk-in closet and private access to the bath

The large living room features a handy coat closet

The kitchen/dining area includes side entrance, closet and convenient laundry area

Price Code AAA

32'-0"

25'-0"

MBr
10-4x12-1

Kit/Din
11-6x12-1

Furn

R

W
D

Br 2
13-2x8-8

Living
15-6x12-0

Porch

© Copyright by designer/architect

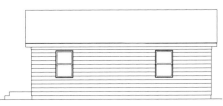

Rear View

To order this plan, visit the Menards Building Materials Desk or visit www.Menards.com.

161

Plan #M07-072L-0274

Open Living Area

1,685 total square feet of living area

4 bedrooms, 3 baths

2-car garage

Basement foundation

Special features

The living and dining rooms create an extra large open space and feature a lovely fireplace, window wall and deck access

The kitchen features a sunny breakfast room with corner windows, and has handy access to the attached double garage through the mud/laundry area

On the second floor, a spacious and vaulted master bedroom with a private bath and a sitting area is flanked by two additional bedrooms and a second full bath

Price Code D

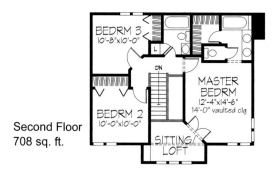

Second Floor
708 sq. ft.

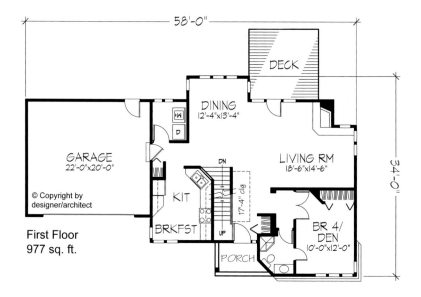

First Floor
977 sq. ft.

To order this plan, visit the *Menards Building Materials Desk* or visit www.Menards.com.

Plan #M07-024L-0010

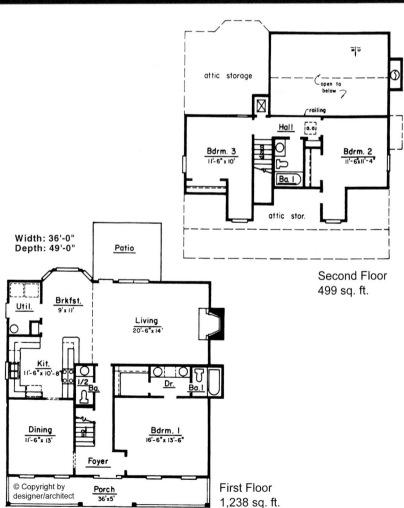

Width: 36'-0"
Depth: 49'-0"

Second Floor
499 sq. ft.

First Floor
1,238 sq. ft.

© Copyright by designer/architect

Quaint Country Home

1,737 total square feet of living area

3 bedrooms, 2 1/2 baths

Slab or crawl space foundation, please specify when ordering

Special features

The U-shaped kitchen, sunny bayed breakfast area and living room become one large gathering area

The living room has a sloped ceiling and a balcony overlook from the second floor

The second floor includes lots of attic storage area

Price Code B

Plan #M07-007D-0040

Apartment Garage
With Surprising Interior

632 total square feet of living area

1 bedroom, 1 bath

2-car garage

Slab foundation

Special features

The porch leads to the vaulted entry and staircase with a feature window, coat closet and access to the garage and laundry closet

The cozy living room offers a vaulted ceiling, fireplace, large palladian window and a pass-through to the kitchen

A garden tub with arched window is part of a very roomy bath

Price Code AAA

Rear View

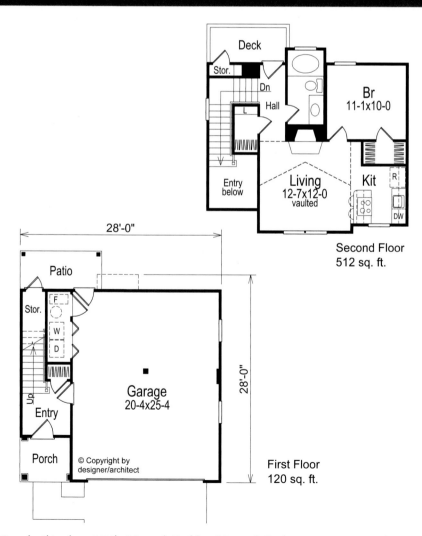

Second Floor
512 sq. ft.

First Floor
120 sq. ft.

To order this plan, visit the Menards Building Materials Desk or visit www.Menards.com.

Plan #M07-001D-0067

Layout Creates
Large Open Living Area

1,285 total square feet of living area

3 bedrooms, 2 baths

Crawl space foundation, drawings also include basement and slab foundations

Special features

This accommodating home has a charming country-style porch

The large storage area on the back of the home is a handy feature

The master bedroom includes a dressing area, private bath and built-in bookcase

The kitchen features a pantry, breakfast bar and complete view to the dining area

2" x 6" exterior walls available, please order plan #M07-001D-0119

Price Code B

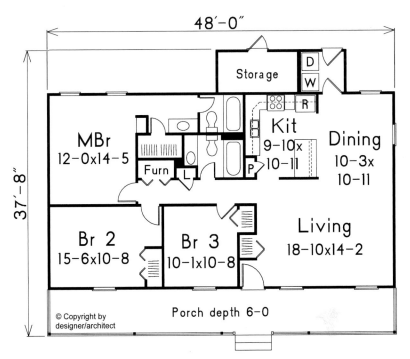

48'-0"

37'-8"

Storage

D W

Kit
9-10x
10-11

Dining
10-3x
10-11

MBr
12-0x14-5

Furn L

P

R

Br 2
15-6x10-8

Br 3
10-1x10-8

Living
18-10x14-2

© Copyright by designer/architect

Porch depth 6-0

Rear View

To order this plan, visit the *Menards* Building Materials Desk or visit www.Menards.com.

165

Plan #M07-007D-0068

Tranquility Of
An Atrium Cottage

1,922 total square feet of living area

2 bedrooms, 2 baths

1-car side entry garage

Walk-out basement foundation

Special features

The wrap-around country porch is perfect for peaceful evenings

The vaulted great room enjoys a large bay window, stone fireplace, pass-through kitchen and awesome rear views through an atrium window wall

The master bedroom features a double-door entry, walk-in closet and a fabulous bath

Price Code B

55'-8"

46'-4"

First Floor
1,415 sq. ft.

- Atrium
- Dining Area
- Kit 10-2x 11-9
- Garage 22-0x11-9
- Great Rm 18-0x21-8 vaulted
- Laun.
- Entry
- Hall
- Porch
- Br 2 11-4x12-6
- MBr 12-8x15-0
- Shelves
- Vaulted

© Copyright by designer/architect

Lower Level
507 sq. ft.

- Up
- Patio
- Family Rm 25-0x21-4
- Unexcavated
- Unfinished Basement

Rear View

To order this plan, visit the *Menards Building Materials Desk* or visit www.Menards.com.

Plan #M07-008D-0134

Rustic Haven

1,275 total square feet of living area

4 bedrooms, 2 baths

Basement foundation, drawings also include crawl space and slab foundations

Special features

Wall shingles and a stone veneer fireplace all fashion an irresistible rustic appeal

The living area features a fireplace and opens to an efficient kitchen

Two bedrooms on the second floor share a full bath

Price Code A

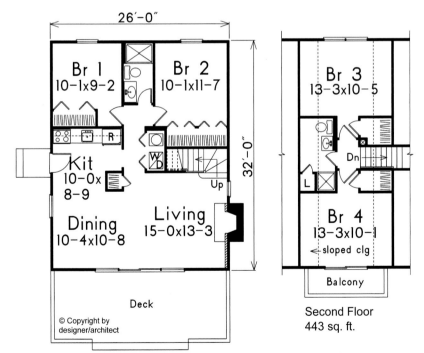

26'-0"

Br 1
10-1x9-2

Br 2
10-1x11-7

Kit
10-0x
8-9

R

W
D

Up

32'-0"

Dining
10-4x10-8

Living
15-0x13-3

Deck

© Copyright by designer/architect

First Floor
832 sq. ft.

Br 3
13-3x10-5

Dn

L

Br 4
13-3x10-1
← sloped clg

Balcony

Second Floor
443 sq. ft.

To order this plan, visit the Menards Building Materials Desk or visit www.Menards.com.

167

Plan #M07-013L-0049

Brick And Planter
Boxes Decorate Front

1,944 total square feet of living area

4 bedrooms, 3 baths

3-car side entry garage

Basement foundation

Special features

The kitchen opens to the nook and dining room for easy meal access

The combined pantry and laundry room connect the home to the garage and workshop

The large master suite has a spacious closet with plenty of room to hang clothes as well as store linens

The sunny guest bedroom with large closet and full bath creates a welcoming room for visitors

Price Code C

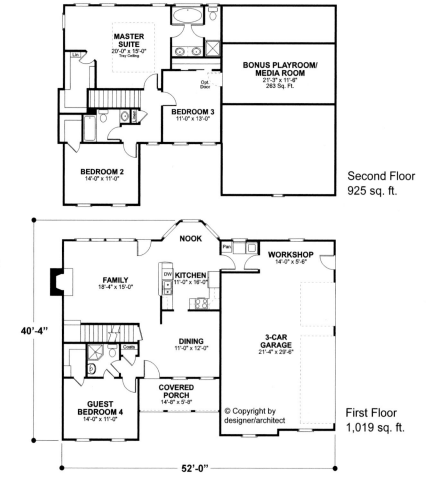

MASTER SUITE
20'-0" x 15'-0"
Tray Ceiling

BONUS PLAYROOM/ MEDIA ROOM
21'-3" x 11'-6"
263 Sq. Ft.

Lin

Opt. Door

Linen

BEDROOM 3
11'-0" x 13'-0"

BEDROOM 2
14'-0" x 11'-0"

Second Floor
925 sq. ft.

40'-4"

NOOK

Pan

WORKSHOP
14'-0" x 5'-6"

FAMILY
18'-4" x 15'-0"

DW **KITCHEN**
11'-0" x 16'-0"

Coats

DINING
11'-0" x 12'-0"

3-CAR GARAGE
21'-4" x 29'-6"

COVERED PORCH
14'-8" x 5'-8"

GUEST BEDROOM 4
14'-0" x 11'-0"

© Copyright by designer/architect

First Floor
1,019 sq. ft.

52'-0"

To order this plan, visit the *Menards* Building Materials Desk or visit www.Menards.com.

MENARDS

Siminridge

Plan #M07-007D-0087

Compact Home For Sloping Lot

1,332 total square feet of living area

3 bedrooms, 2 baths

4-car tandem drive under garage

Walk-out basement foundation

Special features

This home offers both basement and first floor entry locations

The living room features a vaulted ceiling, fireplace, exterior balcony and dining area

An L-shaped kitchen offers spacious cabinetry, breakfast area with bay window and access to the rear patio

2" x 6" exterior walls available, please order plan #M07-007E-0087

Price Code A

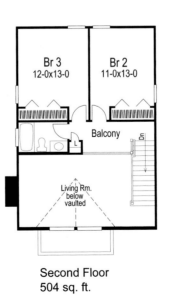

First Floor
828 sq. ft.

30'-6"

40'-0"

Patio

Kit
11-0x12-3

Br 1
12-0x13-0

Entry

Din

Din

Living Rm.
19-4x12-0
vaulted

Balcony

© Copyright by designer/architect

Garage Below

Second Floor
504 sq. ft.

Br 3
12-0x13-0

Br 2
11-0x13-0

Balcony

Living Rm.
below
vaulted

Rear View

Plan #M07-008D-0151

A Home Designed For Hillside Views

1,806 total square feet of living area

3 bedrooms, 2 baths

Walk-out basement foundation

Special features

The wrap-around deck, great for entertaining, enhances this home's appearance

The side entry foyer accesses two rear bedrooms, a hall bath, and the living and dining areas

The L-shaped kitchen is open to the dining area

Lots of living area is provided on the lower level, including a spacious family room with a fireplace and sliding doors to the patio under the deck

The future room on the lower level has an additional 322 square feet of living area

Price Code C

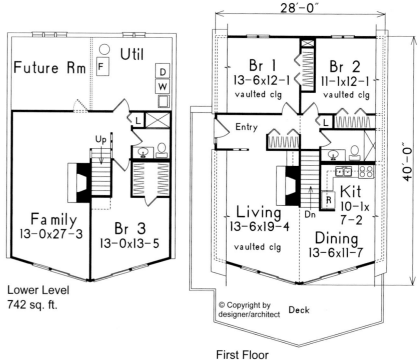

Lower Level
742 sq. ft.

First Floor
1,064 sq. ft.

To order this plan, visit the Menards Building Materials Desk or visit www.Menards.com.

Plan #M07-013L-0043

A Lovely Layout For Casual Family Living

1,343 total square feet of living area

3 bedrooms, 2 baths

2-car garage

Basement or slab foundation, please specify when ordering

Special features

A large front window and high ceiling create an open family room

The kitchen has plenty of counterspace for dining and preparing food

A screened porch is connected to the master suite for an open air feel

The laundry room is centrally located between all the bedrooms

Price Code B

SCREENED PORCH
13'-1" x 9'-7"

MASTER SUITE
13' x 14'-4"
12' Ceiling

BEDROOM 2
11' x 11'

BEDROOM 3
11'-8" x 10'-6"

© Copyright by designer/architect

Coats

2-CAR FRONT-LOAD GARAGE
22' x 20'

Pantry

Dn

KITCHEN
16' x 9'

DW

DINING
11' x 11'

FAMILY
15' x 16'
12' Ceiling

PORCH
10'-11" x 7'-8"

60'-0"

28'-0"

50'-0"

To order this plan, visit the Menards Building Materials Desk or visit www.Menards.com.

171

Plan #M07-007D-0189

Apartment Garage Plus RV Storage

713 total square feet of living area

1 bedroom, 1 1/2 baths

2-car garage, RV garage

Slab foundation

Special features

The living room features a bayed dining area and a separate entry with access to the garage and the staircase to the second floor

A very efficient and well-equipped L-shaped kitchen has a view to the rear yard and a built-in pantry

The second floor offers a large bedroom with alcove for a desk, walk-in closet and a private bath off the hall

Price Code AAA

Rear View

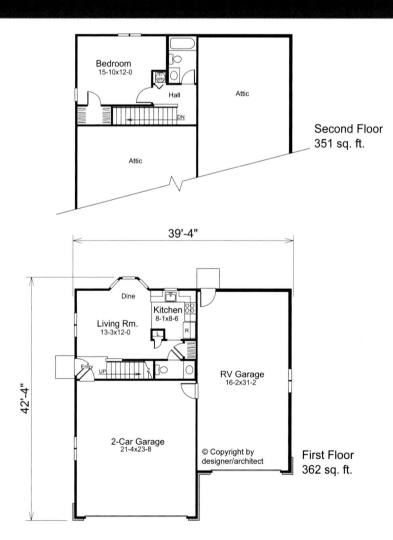

Second Floor
351 sq. ft.

Bedroom
15-10x12-0

Hall

Attic

Attic

First Floor
362 sq. ft.

Dine

Kitchen
8-1x8-6

Living Rm.
13-3x12-0

Entry

UP

RV Garage
16-2x31-2

2-Car Garage
21-4x23-8

© Copyright by designer/architect

39'-4"

42'-4"

To order this plan, visit the Menards Building Materials Desk or visit www.Menards.com.

Plan #M07-001D-0055

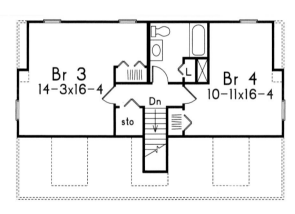

Second Floor
665 sq. ft.

Plenty Of Room For A Growing Family

1,705 total square feet of living area

4 bedrooms, 2 baths

Crawl space foundation, drawings also include basement and slab foundations

Special features

There are two bedrooms on the first floor for convenience and two bedrooms on the second floor for privacy

The L-shaped kitchen is adjacent to the dining room

2" x 6" exterior walls available, please order plan #M07-001D-0110

Price Code B

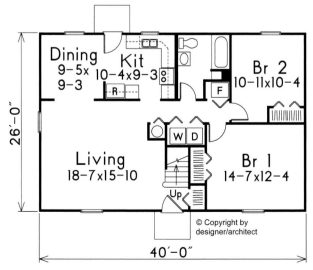

First Floor
1,040 sq. ft.

© Copyright by designer/architect

Rear View

To order this plan, visit the Menards Building Materials Desk or visit www.Menards.com.

173

Plan #M07-058D-0013

Comfortable Vacation Retreat

1,073 total square feet of living area

2 bedrooms, 1 bath

Crawl space foundation

Special features

This home includes a lovely covered front porch and a screened porch off the dining area

An attractive box window brightens the kitchen

Space for an efficiency washer and dryer is located conveniently between the bedrooms

The family room includes a fireplace with flanking bookshelves and a spacious vaulted ceiling

Price Code AA

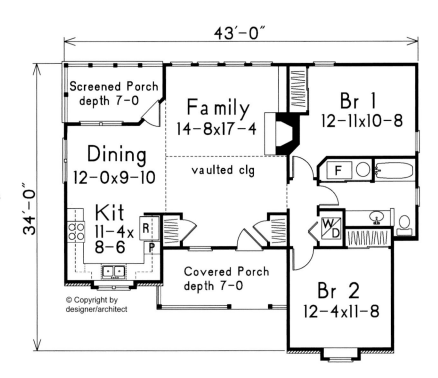

43'-0"

34'-0"

Screened Porch
depth 7-0

Family
14-8x17-4

Br 1
12-11x10-8

Dining
12-0x9-10

vaulted clg

Kit
11-4x
8-6

R
P

F

W
D

Covered Porch
depth 7-0

Br 2
12-4x11-8

© Copyright by
designer/architect

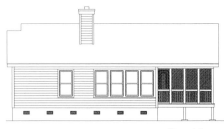

Rear View

To order this plan, visit the Menards Building Materials Desk or visit www.Menards.com.

Plan #M07-001D-0018

Front Porch And Center Gable Add Style To This Ranch

988 total square feet of living area

3 bedrooms, 1 bath

1-car garage

Basement foundation, drawings also include crawl space foundation

Special features

This home has a pleasant covered porch entry

The kitchen, living and dining areas are combined to maximize space

The entry has a convenient coat closet

The laundry closet is located adjacent to the bedrooms

Price Code AA

Floor plan labels:

- Br 1 — 11-6x12-4
- Kit — 8-1x8-3
- Dining — 12-0x10-1
- Br 2 — 11-6x10-2
- Br 3 — 8-8x10-2
- Living — 14-3x15-4
- Garage — 11-8x25-5
- Porch depth 4-0
- 26'-0"
- 50'-0"
- © Copyright by designer/architect

Rear View

Sabrina

To order this plan, visit the Menards Building Materials Desk or visit www.Menards.com.

Plan #M07-017D-0007

Pillared Front Porch Generates Charm And Warmth

1,567 total square feet of living area

3 bedrooms, 2 baths

2-car side entry garage

Partial basement/crawl space foundation, drawings also include slab foundation

Special features

Energy efficient home with 2" x 6" exterior walls

The living room flows into the dining area

The cheerful, windowed dining area has terrace access

The master bedroom is separated from the other bedrooms for privacy

Future area available on the second floor has an additional 338 square feet of living area

Price Code C

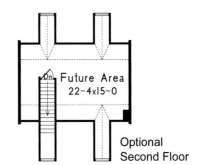

Future Area
22-4x15-0

Optional
Second Floor

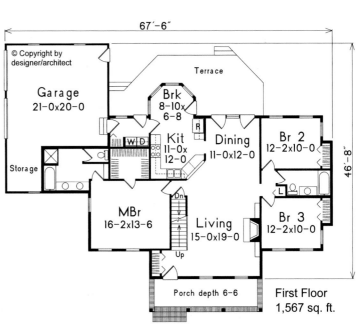

67'-6"

© Copyright by designer/architect

Terrace

Garage
21-0x20-0

Brk
8-10x
6-8

Kit
11-0x
12-0

Dining
11-0x12-0

Br 2
12-2x10-0

Storage

W D

R

MBr
16-2x13-6

Dn

Living
15-0x19-0

Br 3
12-2x10-0

Up

46'-8"

Porch depth 6-6

First Floor
1,567 sq. ft.

Rear View

Plan #M07-007D-0137

Country Lodge With Screened Porch And Fireplace

1,568 total square feet of living area

2 bedrooms, 2 baths

3-car side entry garage

Crawl space foundation

Special features

Multiple entrances from three porches help to bring the outdoors in

The lodge-like great room features a vaulted ceiling, stone fireplace, step-up entrance foyer and opens to a huge screened porch

The kitchen has an island and peninsula, a convenient laundry area and adjoins a spacious dining area that leads to a screened porch and rear patio

The master bedroom has two walk-in closets, a luxury bath and access to the screened porch and patio

Price Code B

72'-8"

44'-4"

Patio

MBr
14-5x13-3
vaulted

Screened Porch
19-3x17-4
vaulted

Dining
12-1x12-0

Boat/Jet Ski
Garage
21-4x12-8

Hall

Kit
12-1x15-0

Garage
21-4x20-4

Br 2
14-1x11-0

Great Room
19-4x25-8
vaulted

Raised
Entry

Laund.
W D

DW

R

© Copyright by
designer/architect

Porch

Porch

Rear View

To order this plan, visit the Menards Building Materials Desk or visit www.Menards.com.

177

Wakefield Forest

Plan #M07-077L-0001

Gables Add Warmth To Exterior

1,638 total square feet of living area

3 bedrooms, 2 baths

2-car side entry garage

Basement, crawl space or slab foundation, please specify when ordering

Special features

The great room features a fireplace with flanking doors that access the covered porch

The centrally located kitchen serves the breakfast and dining areas with ease

There is plenty of storage space located in the garage

Price Code D

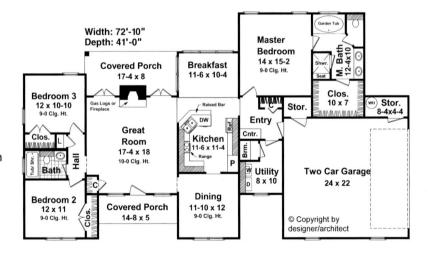

Width: 72'-10"
Depth: 41'-0"

Bedroom 3
12 x 10-10
9-0 Clg. Ht.

Covered Porch
17-4 x 8

Breakfast
11-6 x 10-4

Master Bedroom
14 x 15-2
9-0 Clg. Ht.

Garden Tub

M. Bath
12-4x10

Shwr.
Seat

Clos.
10 x 7

Stor.
8-4x4-4

WH

Clos.

Gas Logs or Fireplace

Raised Bar

DW

Ref.

Entry

Stor.

Great Room
17-4 x 18
10-0 Clg. Ht.

Kitchen
11-6 x 11-4

Range

Cntr.

Brm.

Hall

Tub/ Shwr.

Bath

P

Two Car Garage
24 x 22

Bedroom 2
12 x 11
9-0 Clg. Ht.

C

Clos.

W
D

Utility
8 x 10

Covered Porch
14-8 x 5

Dining
11-10 x 12
9-0 Clg. Ht.

© Copyright by designer/architect

Down

Clos.
10 x 7

Stor.
8-4x4-4

WH

Entry

Brm.

W
D

Utility
8 x 10

Two Car Garage
24 x 22

Optional Stair Location

Plan #M07-001D-0072

Peaceful Shaded Front Porch

1,288 total square feet of living area

3 bedrooms, 2 baths

Crawl space foundation, drawings also include basement and slab foundations

Special features

The kitchen, dining area and great room join to create an open living space

The master bedroom includes a private bath

The secondary bedrooms enjoy ample closet space

The hall bath features a convenient laundry closet

The dining room accesses the outdoors

Price Code A

46'-0"

28'-0"

MBr
15-9x14-7

Kit
8-1x
11-4

Dining
9-8x
14-11

W
D

Furn

R

Br 2
13-9x10-1

Br 3
11-8x9-0

Great Rm
17-0x12-6

© Copyright by designer/architect

Porch depth 4-0

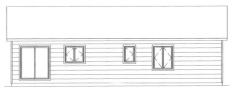

Rear View

To order this plan, visit the Menards Building Materials Desk or visit www.Menards.com.

179

Paige

Plan #M07-121D-0016

Charming Country Cottage

1,582 total square feet of living area

3 bedrooms, 2 baths

2-car detached garage

Basement foundation

Special features

The wrap-around covered front porch is perfect for relaxing and enjoying the outdoors

Vaulted ceilings throughout this home provide an open and airy atmosphere

The kitchen boasts a large walk-in pantry and ample counterspace with an eating bar for convenient meals

Price Code A

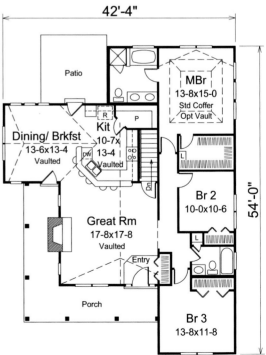

24'-0"

Detached Garage
23-4x23-4

© Copyright by designer/architect

24'-0"

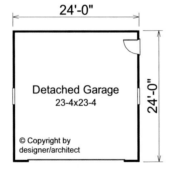

42'-4"

Patio

Dining/ Brkfst
13-6x13-4
Vaulted

Kit
10-7x
13-4
Vaulted

MBr
13-8x15-0
Std Coffer
Opt Vault

Great Rm
17-8x17-8
Vaulted

Br 2
10-0x10-6

Entry

Porch

Br 3
13-8x11-8

54'-0"

Rear View

Plan #M07-053D-0058

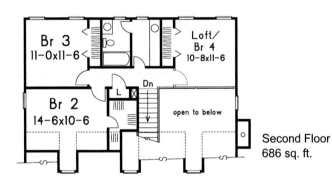

Second Floor
686 sq. ft.

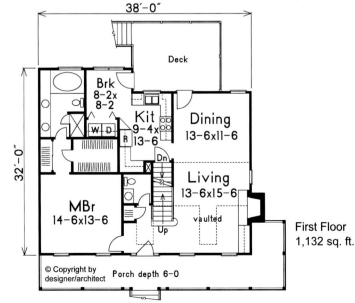

First Floor
1,132 sq. ft.

© Copyright by designer/architect   Porch depth 6-0

Lovely Country Home

1,818 total square feet of living area

4 bedrooms, 2 1/2 baths

2-car drive under side entry garage

Walk-out basement foundation

Special features

The breakfast room is tucked behind the kitchen and has a laundry closet

The living and dining areas share a vaulted ceiling and fireplace

The master bedroom has two closets, a large double-bowl vanity and a separate tub

The lower level has an additional 599 square feet of living area

Price Code A

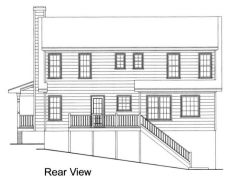

Rear View

To order this plan, visit the *Menards Building Materials Desk* or visit www.Menards.com.

181

Plan #M07-058D-0085

Rustic Design With Modern Features

1,000 total square feet of living area

2 bedrooms, 1 bath

Crawl space foundation

Special features

Energy efficient home with 2" x 6" exterior walls

The large mud room has a separate covered porch entrance

This home has a full-length covered front porch

The bedrooms are on opposite sides of the home for privacy

The vaulted ceilings in the family and dining areas create an open and spacious feeling

Price Code AA

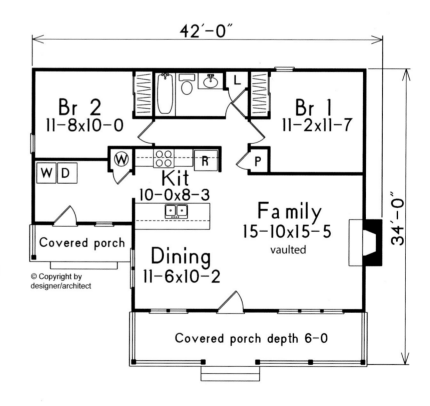

42'-0"

Br 2
11-8x10-0

Br 1
11-2x11-7

L

W

R

P

W D

Kit
10-0x8-3

Covered porch

Family
15-10x15-5
vaulted

34'-0"

Dining
11-6x10-2

© Copyright by
designer/architect

Covered porch depth 6-0

Plan #M07-068D-0006

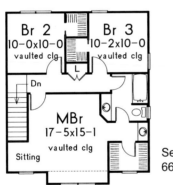

Br 2
10-0x10-0
vaulted clg

Br 3
10-2x10-0
vaulted clg

L

Dn

MBr
17-5x15-1
vaulted clg

Sitting

Second Floor
667 sq. ft.

Covered Porch Surrounds Home

1,399 total square feet of living area

3 bedrooms, 1 1/2 baths

1-car garage

Basement foundation, drawings also include crawl space and slab foundations

Special features

The living room overlooks the dining area through arched columns

The laundry room contains a handy half bath

The spacious master bedroom includes a sitting area, walk-in closet and plenty of sunlight

Price Code A

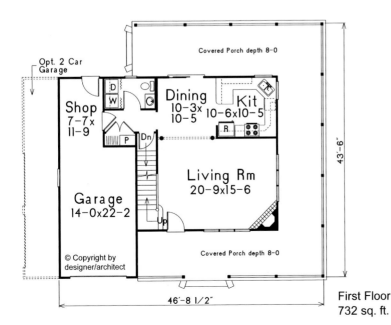

Covered Porch depth 8-0

Opt. 2 Car
Garage

Shop
7-7 x
11-9

D
W

Dining
10-3x
10-5

Kit
10-6x10-5

R

Dn

P

Living Rm
20-9x15-6

Garage
14-0x22-2

© Copyright by
designer/architect

Covered Porch depth 8-0

43'-6"

46'-8 1/2"

First Floor
732 sq. ft.

Rear View

To order this plan, visit the *Menards* Building Materials Desk or visit www.Menards.com.

183

Haviland

Plan #M07-058D-0151

2-Car Garage Apartment

973 total square feet of living area

2 bedrooms, 1 bath

2-car side entry garage with storage

Basement foundation

Special features

The side entry garage makes this apartment garage look like a two-story home

The sunny breakfast room is positioned between the kitchen and the family room for convenience

Both bedrooms are generously sized

Price Code AAA

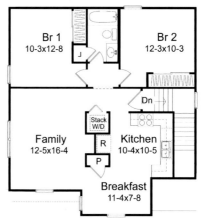

Second Floor
973 sq. ft.

Br 1
10-3x12-8

Br 2
12-3x10-3

Family
12-5x16-4

Stack W/D

Kitchen
10-4x10-5

Dn

Breakfast
11-4x7-8

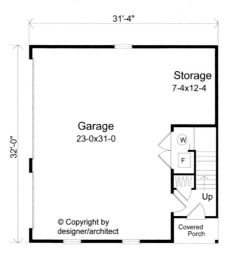

31'-4"

32'-0"

Garage
23-0x31-0

Storage
7-4x12-4

Up

Covered Porch

© Copyright by designer/architect

First Floor

Plan #M07-001D-0085

Designed For Comfort And Utility

720 total square feet of living area

2 bedrooms, 1 bath

Crawl space foundation, drawings also include slab foundation

Special features

Abundant windows in the living and dining rooms provide generous sunlight

The secluded laundry area has a handy storage closet

The U-shaped kitchen with large breakfast bar opens into the living area

The large covered porch offers plenty of outdoor living space

Price Code AAA

24'-0"

30'-0"

Br 1
11-6x10-8

Br 2
9-2x 9-5

L

D W

Kit

Living
12-2x13-0

Dining
11-3x13-0

Covered Porch depth 8-0

© Copyright by designer/architect

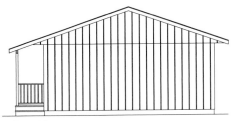

Rear View

To order this plan, visit the Menards Building Materials Desk or visit www.Menards.com.

185

Coburg Manor

MENARDS

Plan #M07-065L-0173

Exciting Two-Story

1,969 total square feet of living area

3 bedrooms, 2 1/2 baths

2-car garage

Basement foundation

Special features

An octagonal tower, covered porch, arched trim and boxed window decorate the exterior

The great room with fireplace, high windows and rear yard access provides an excellent atmosphere for family activities

The dramatic views to the great room and foyer are provided at the second floor balcony where there is ample room for a computer area or reading loft

The second floor bonus room has an additional 268 square feet of living space

Price Code C

Second Floor 549 sq. ft.

First Floor 1,420 sq. ft.

Width: 58'-0"
Depth: 44'-4"

© Copyright by designer/architect

Plan #M07-041D-0005

Gables Accent This Home

1,239 total square feet of living area

3 bedrooms, 2 1/2 baths

2-car garage

Basement foundation

Special features

The master bedroom has a private bath and walk-in closet

A convenient coat closet and pantry are located near the garage entrance

The dining area accesses the deck

The stairway with sloped ceiling creates an open atmosphere in the great room

Price Code A

Second Floor 386 sq. ft.

Br 3
10-6x
8-6

Br 2
9-6x
11-0

L

Dn

sloped ceiling

Deck

Kit
10-2x
13-0

Dining
9-4x13-8

MBr
11-0x13-6

Dn

P

Great Rm
15-2x15-6

Up

Garage
20-0x24-0

Porch

First Floor 853 sq. ft.

36'-8"

47'-0"

© Copyright by designer/architect

Rear View

To order this plan, visit the *Menards Building Materials Desk* or visit www.Menards.com.

187

Grass Roots 1

MENARDS

To order this plan, visit the Menards Building Materials Desk or visit www.Menards.com.

Plan #M07-001D-0041

Open Living Space Creates Comfortable Atmosphere

1,000 total square feet of living area

3 bedrooms, 1 bath

Crawl space foundation, drawings also include basement and slab foundations

Special features

The bathroom includes a convenient closeted laundry area

The master bedroom includes double closets and private access to the bath

The foyer features a handy coat closet

The kitchen/dining area provides easy access outdoors

Price Code AA

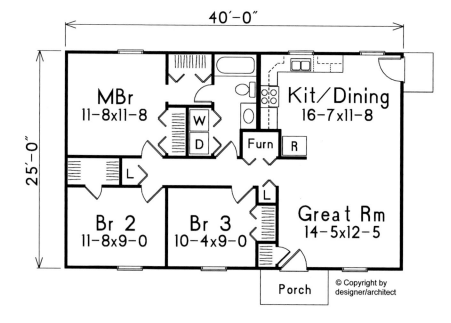

MBr 11-8x11-8

Kit/Dining 16-7x11-8

Br 2 11-8x9-0

Br 3 10-4x9-0

Great Rm 14-5x12-5

Furn

Porch

© Copyright by designer/architect

40'-0"

25'-0"

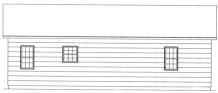

Rear View

MENARDS

Ellistown

Plan #M07-024L-0014

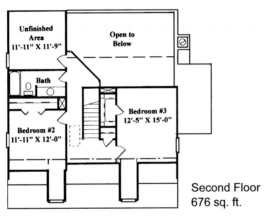

Second Floor
676 sq. ft.

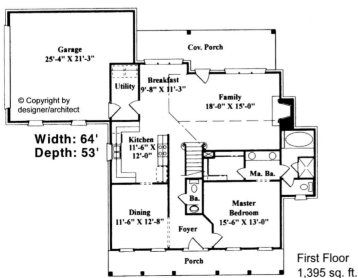

Width: 64'
Depth: 53'

First Floor
1,395 sq. ft.

Three Or Four Bedrooms

2,071 total square feet of living area

3 bedrooms, 2 1/2 baths

2-car side entry garage

Slab or crawl space foundation, please specify when ordering

Special features

The vaulted family room features a cozy fireplace

The sunny breakfast area is brightened by triple windows

The private dining room is perfect for entertaining

The second floor includes two bedrooms, a bath and an unfinished area that offers an additional 149 of living area

Price Code C

To order this plan, visit the Menards Building Materials Desk or visit www.Menards.com.

189

Charlemagne

Plan #M07-058D-0058

Window Brightens Living Room

1,865 total square feet of living area

3 bedrooms, 2 1/2 baths

2-car garage

Basement foundation

Special features

The family room, breakfast area and kitchen combine forming a large open area for family activities

A double-door entry leads to the grand master bedroom that includes two walk-in closets and a private bath

Bedrooms #2 and #3 enjoy walk-in closets and share a bath

Price Code C

Rear View

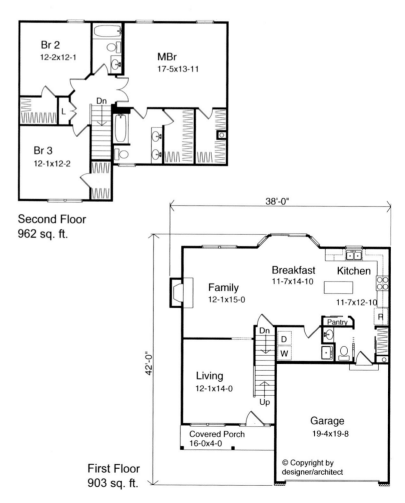

Second Floor
962 sq. ft.

First Floor
903 sq. ft.

© Copyright by designer/architect

To order this plan, visit the *Menards* Building Materials Desk or visit *www.Menards.com.*

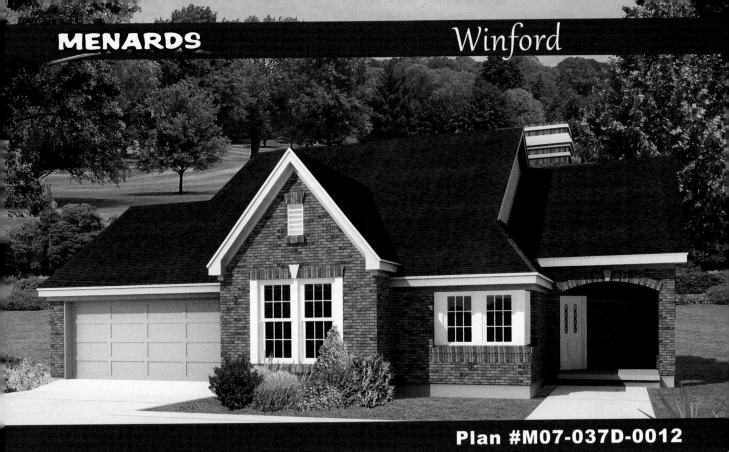

Plan #M07-037D-0012

Sheltered Entrance
Opens To Stylish Features

1,661 total square feet of living area

3 bedrooms, 2 baths

2-car garage

Slab foundation

Special features

The large open foyer with angled wall and high ceiling adds to the spacious living room

The kitchen and dining area have impressive cathedral ceilings and a French door allowing access to the rear porch

A utility room is located near the kitchen

The secluded master bedroom has a large walk-in closet, unique brick wall arrangement and 10' ceiling

Price Code B

Rear View

Floor plan dimensions:

52'-0"

58'-4"

Dining 13-0x11-0 vaulted

Porch

MBr 13-4x15-0

Kit 13-0x11-0

Living 14-4x20-4

Foyer

Porch

Garage 19-8x22-4

© Copyright by designer/architect

Br 2 11-0x12-0

Br 3 10-0x12-0

To order this plan, visit the Menards Building Materials Desk or visit www.Menards.com.

191

Hatteras II

MENARDS

Plan #M07-001D-0056

Front Dormers Add Light And Space

1,705 total square feet of living area

4 bedrooms, 2 baths

Crawl space foundation, drawings also include basement and slab foundations

Special features

This cozy design includes two bedrooms on the first floor and two bedrooms on the second floor for added privacy

The L-shaped kitchen provides easy access to the dining room and the outdoors

This home has a convenient first floor laundry area

2" x 6" exterior walls available, please order plan #M07-001D-0111

Price Code B

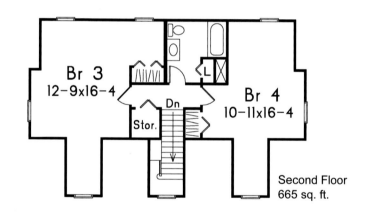

Br 3
12-9x16-4

Br 4
10-11x16-4

Dn

Stor.

Second Floor
665 sq. ft.

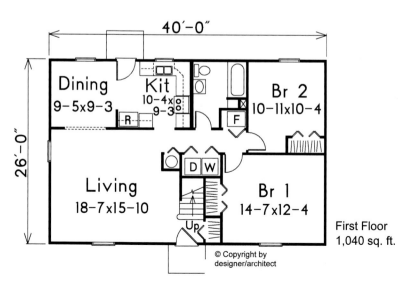

40'-0"

26'-0"

Dining
9-5x9-3

Kit
10-4x
9-3

Br 2
10-11x10-4

Living
18-7x15-10

Br 1
14-7x12-4

© Copyright by designer/architect

First Floor
1,040 sq. ft.

Rear View

To order this plan, visit the *Menards* Building Materials Desk or visit *www.Menards.com.*

Plan #M07-057D-0019

Stone Decorates Facade

1,838 total square feet of living area

3 bedrooms, 2 baths

2-car garage

Crawl space foundation, drawings also include basement foundation

Special features

Energy efficient home with 2" x 6" exterior walls

The angled great room features a corner fireplace, French doors to the rear deck and connects to the dining room for a spacious atmosphere

The wrap-around kitchen counter offers plenty of workspace and room for casual meals

Retreat to the master bedroom where a deluxe bath, walk-in closets and deck access will pamper the homeowners

Price Code C

Floor plan dimensions and labels:

52'-0"

53'-8"

- DECK
- Kit 13-10x17-2
- R
- P
- Dining 11-2x13-0
- MBr 15-1x15-4
- L'DRY
- Great Rm 18-1x21-4
- Garage 21-7x23-7
- Br 1 10-7x12-2
- Br 2/ Study 11-2x12-0
- PORCH 6-10x6-4

© Copyright by designer/architect

To order this plan, visit the Menards Building Materials Desk or visit www.Menards.com.

193

Plan #M07-077L-0081

Open Floor Plan

1,818 total square feet of living area

3 bedrooms, 3 baths

2-car side entry garage

Basement foundation

Special features

Useful and beautiful cabinetry flanks a center fireplace in the vaulted great room

A highly functional screen porch will be enjoyed year round

A corner whirlpool tub highlights the master bath, along with a walk-in closet and double-bowl vanity

Price Code D

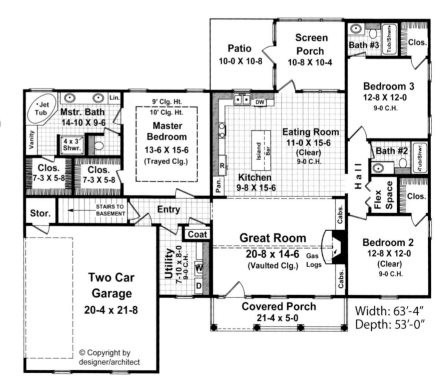

Width: 63'-4"
Depth: 53'-0"

To order this plan, visit the Menards Building Materials Desk or visit www.Menards.com.

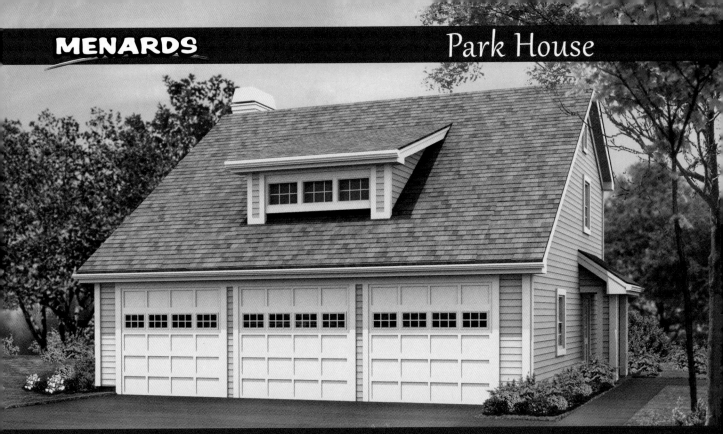

Plan #M07-007D-0145

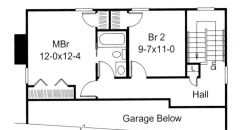

MBr 12-0x12-4

Br 2 9-7x11-0

Hall

Dn

Garage Below

Second Floor 492 sq. ft.

Three-Car Apartment Garage

1,005 total square feet of living area

2 bedrooms, 1 1/2 baths

3-car garage

Slab foundation

Special features

The side porch leads to an entry hall that accesses the living room, U-shaped kitchen, powder room and staircase to the second floor

The large living room has a fireplace, sliding doors to the rear patio, dining area with bay window and opens to the kitchen

The second floor is comprised of two bedrooms and a bath

Price Code AAA

40'-0"

Patio

Din

Kit 8-8x 8-8

DW

R

Living Rm. 18-6x12-8

(WH)

Up

Entry

Porch

38'-0"

W/D

3-Car Garage 34-0x22-4

© Copyright by designer/architect

First Floor 513 sq. ft.

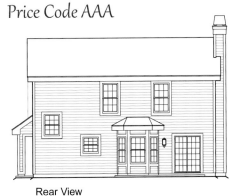

Rear View

To order this plan, visit the Menards Building Materials Desk or visit www.Menards.com.

195

Plan #M07-013L-0136

Lovely Family Area

1,831 total square feet of living area

3 bedrooms, 2 1/2 baths

2-car side entry garage

Slab foundation

Special features

Raised ceilings, arch-top windows, a fireplace and decorative columns add drama to the combined family and dining rooms

This split-bedroom design offers a master suite complete with a tray ceiling, plush bath and sitting area that accesses the screened porch

Two bonus rooms on the second floor offer an additional 798 square feet of living space that can be finished as needed

Price Code C

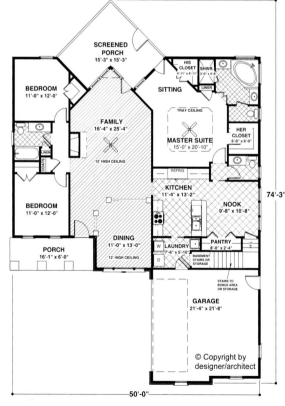

First Floor
1,831 sq. ft.

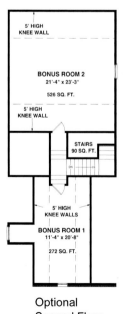

Optional
Second Floor

To order this plan, visit the Menards Building Materials Desk or visit www.Menards.com.

Plan #M07-053D-0007

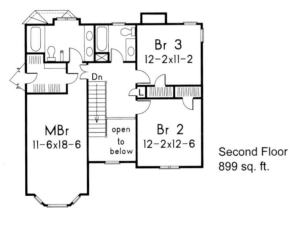

Second Floor
899 sq. ft.

Two-Story Foyer Adds To Country Charm

1,922 total square feet of living area

3 bedrooms, 2 1/2 baths

2-car garage

Walk-out basement foundation

Special features

This home's varied front elevation features numerous accents

The master bedroom suite is well-secluded with a double-door entry and private bath

The formal living and dining rooms are located off the entry

Price Code A

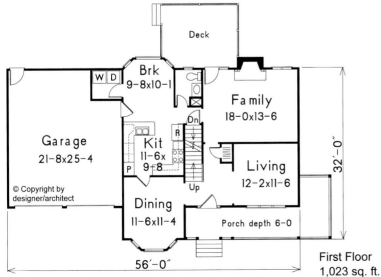

© Copyright by designer/architect

First Floor
1,023 sq. ft.

Rear View

To order this plan, visit the Menards Building Materials Desk or visit www.Menards.com.

197

Plan #M07-007D-0134

Affordable Simplicity

1,310 total square feet of living area

3 bedrooms, 2 baths

2-car garage

Basement foundation, drawings also include crawl space and slab foundations

Special features

The combination of brick quoins, roof dormers and an elegant porch creates a classic look

Open floor plan has vaulted kitchen, living and dining rooms

The master bedroom is vaulted and enjoys privacy from the other bedrooms

A spacious laundry room is convenient to the kitchen and master bedroom with access to an oversized garage

2" x 6" exterior walls available, please order plan #M07-007E-0134

Price Code A

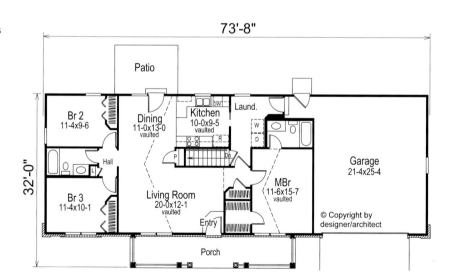

Rear View

Plan #M07-008D-0143

Breathtaking Balcony Overlook

1,299 total square feet of living area

3 bedrooms, 2 baths

Crawl space foundation, drawings also include slab foundation

Special features

A convenient storage area for skis and other equipment is located outside the rear entrance

The kitchen and dining room receive light from the box-bay window

The large vaulted living room features a cozy fireplace and overlook from the second floor balcony

Two second floor bedrooms share a Jack and Jill bath

The second floor balcony extends over the entire length of the living room below

Price Code A

28'-0"

Deck

Stor

R

Br 1
9-11x11-6

Kit
10-7x
8-3

D
W

Din
10-10x
7-3

Living
23-10x12-3

Up

46'-0"

Deck

© Copyright by designer/architect

First Floor
811 sq. ft.

Deck

Br 2
11-2x11-6

Br 3
10-6x11-6

Balcony

Dn

open to below

Second Floor
488 sq. ft.

To order this plan, visit the *Menards Building Materials Desk* or visit www.Menards.com.

199

Plan #M07-121D-0012

Small Home Packed With Big Style

1,281 total square feet of living area

3 bedrooms, 2 baths

2-car garage

Basement foundation

Special features

The well-appointed kitchen enjoys an angled raised counter perfect for casual dining

The great room has an 11' ceiling, a fireplace for warmth, and easy access to the breakfast area

The vaulted master bedroom enjoys a sizable walk-in closet and its own private bath

Price Code AA

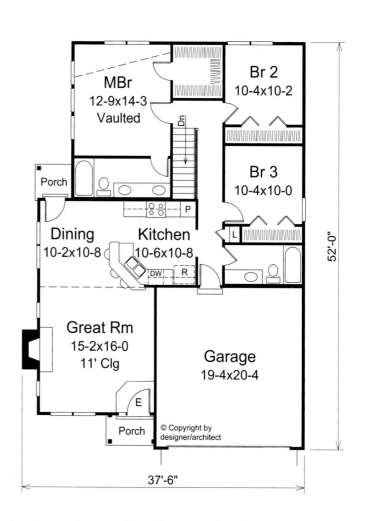

MBr
12-9x14-3
Vaulted

Br 2
10-4x10-2

Porch

Dn

Br 3
10-4x10-0

Dining
10-2x10-8

Kitchen
10-6x10-8

P

DW   R

L

Great Rm
15-2x16-0
11' Clg

Garage
19-4x20-4

E

Porch

© Copyright by
designer/architect

52'-0"

37'-6"

Rear View

Birkhill

Plan #M07-007D-0148

Hall

MBr
12-0x14-7

Br 2
11-7x14-0

Second Floor
691 sq. ft.

28'-0"

30'-0"

Patio

W D P **Brk fst**
10-0x10-0

Laun.

DW

Kit
7-3x8-0

R

Dn

Garage
12-0x21-0

Living
11-7x15-0

Up

E

© Copyright by
designer/architect

Porch

First Floor
476 sq. ft.

Compact Two-Story Home

1,167 total square feet of living area

2 bedrooms, 2 1/2 baths

1-car garage

Basement foundation

Special features

The sizable living room features a separate entry foyer and view to the front porch

The functional kitchen has a breakfast room with bay window, built-in pantry and a laundry room with a half bath

The master bedroom offers three closets and a luxury bath

Price Code AA

Rear View

To order this plan, visit the *Menards Building Materials Desk* or visit *www.Menards.com*.

201

Plan #M07-022D-0022

Perfect Fit For A Narrow Site

1,270 total square feet of living area

3 bedrooms, 2 baths

2-car garage

Basement foundation

Special features

The spacious living area features an angled staircase, a vaulted ceiling, an exciting fireplace and deck access

The master bedroom includes a walk-in closet and private bath

The dining and living rooms join to create an open atmosphere

The eat-in kitchen has a convenient pass-through to the dining room

Price Code A

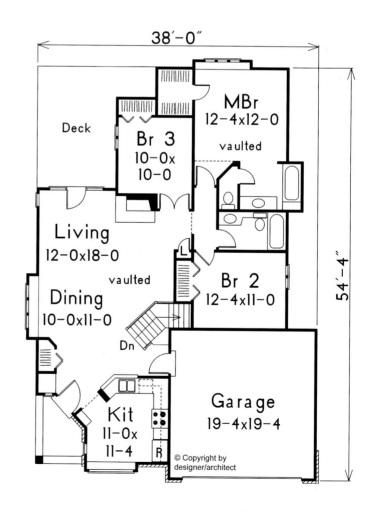

38'-0"

54'-4"

Deck

MBr
12-4x12-0
vaulted

Br 3
10-0x
10-0

Living
12-0x18-0
vaulted

Br 2
12-4x11-0

Dining
10-0x11-0

Dn

Kit
11-0x
11-4

Garage
19-4x19-4

© Copyright by designer/architect

Rear View

Plan #M07-001D-0039

Perfect Home
For A Small Family

864 total square feet of living area

2 bedrooms, 1 bath

Crawl space foundation, drawings also include basement and slab foundations

Special features

The L-shaped kitchen with convenient pantry is adjacent to the dining area

This home has easy access to the laundry, linen and storage closets

Both bedrooms include ample closet space

Price Code AAA

36'-0"

24'-0"

Br 1
13-2x10-1

Kit
10-2x6-8

D W Furn

Dining
9-5x 10-4

Br 2
11-8x13-0

L L

Living
13-5x13-0

R

© Copyright by designer/architect

4-0 Porch depth

Rear View

To order this plan, visit the *Menards* Building Materials Desk or visit www.Menards.com.

203

Plan #M07-068D-0005

Spacious Living In This Ranch

1,433 total square feet of living area

3 bedrooms, 2 baths

2-car garage

Basement foundation, drawings also include crawl space and slab foundations

Special features

The vaulted living room includes a cozy fireplace and an oversized entertainment center

Bedrooms #2 and #3 share a full bath

The master bedroom has a full bath and large walk-in closet

Price Code A

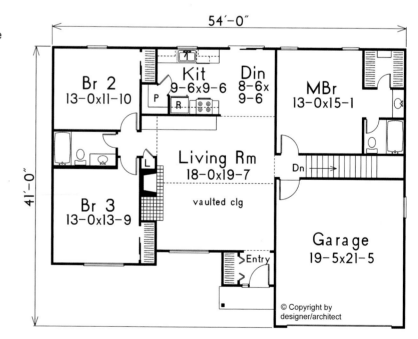

54'-0"

41'-0"

Br 2
13-0x11-10

Kit
9-6x9-6

Din
8-6x
9-6

MBr
13-0x15-1

Living Rm
18-0x19-7
vaulted clg

Br 3
13-0x13-9

Dn

Garage
19-5x21-5

Entry

© Copyright by designer/architect

Rear View

To order this plan, visit the Menards Building Materials Desk or visit www.Menards.com.

Plan #M07-024L-0046

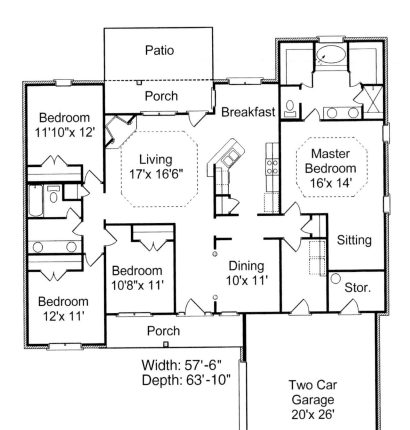

Tranquil Master Bedroom

2,208 total square feet of living area

4 bedrooms, 2 baths

2-car side entry garage

Slab foundation

Special features

The kitchen counter with seating opens to the spacious living room which features a corner fireplace and access to the rear porch

Decorative columns adorn the dining room entry

The master bedroom sitting area is a quiet place to relax

Price Code C

To order this plan, visit the Menards Building Materials Desk or visit www.Menards.com.

205

MENARDS

Plan #M07-058D-0020

Surrounding Country Porch

1,428 total square feet of living area

3 bedrooms, 2 baths

Basement foundation

Special features

The large vaulted family room opens to the dining area and kitchen with breakfast bar

First floor master bedroom offers a bath, walk-in closet and nearby laundry facilities

A spacious loft/bedroom #3 overlooking the family room and an additional bedroom and bath complement the second floor

2" x 6" exterior walls available, please order plan #M07-058D-0080

Price Code A

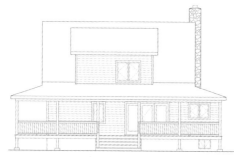

Rear View

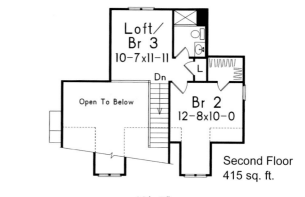

Second Floor
415 sq. ft.

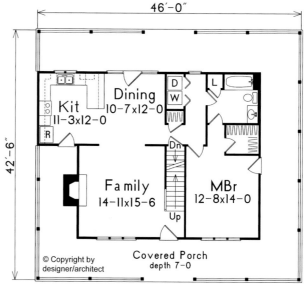

First Floor
1,013 sq. ft.

206

Plan #M07-001D-0093

Convenient Ranch

1,120 total square feet of living area

3 bedrooms, 1 1/2 baths

Crawl space foundation, drawings also include basement and slab foundations

Special features

The master bedroom includes a half bath with laundry area, linen closet and kitchen access

The kitchen has a charming double-door entry, a breakfast bar and a convenient walk-in pantry

The welcoming front porch opens to a large living room with coat closet

Price Code AA

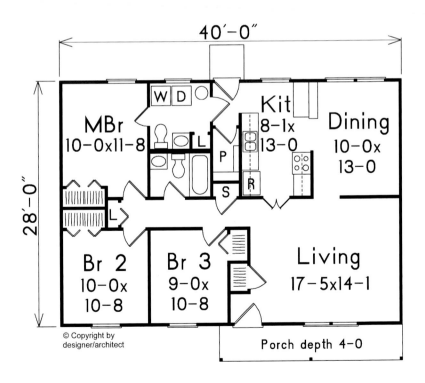

40'-0"

28'-0"

MBr 10-0x11-8

W D

Kit 8-1x 13-0

Dining 10-0x 13-0

P
S R
L

Br 2 10-0x 10-8

Br 3 9-0x 10-8

Living 17-5x14-1

© Copyright by designer/architect

Porch depth 4-0

Rear View

To order this plan, visit the Menards Building Materials Desk or visit www.Menards.com.

207

Plan #M07-077L-0105

Compact And Stylish Design

1,100 total square feet of living area

2 bedrooms, 2 baths

Slab foundation

Special features

This home is designed with insulated concrete formed exterior walls providing a tighter construction, conserving heating and cooling energy consumption

The two bedrooms are larger than you would expect for a house of this size, and one includes a private bath with a whirlpool tub

A separate laundry room, pantry, linen and hall closet add convenient storage and workspace to this design

Relax with friends and family on either the front or rear covered porches

Price Code C

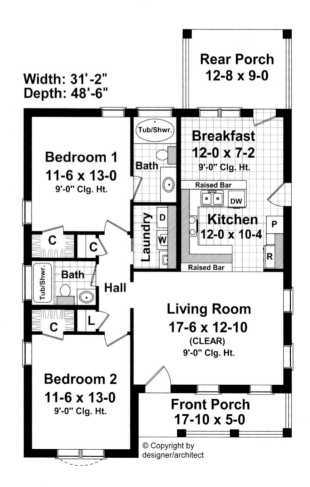

Width: 31'-2"
Depth: 48'-6"

Rear Porch
12-8 x 9-0

Bedroom 1
11-6 x 13-0
9'-0" Clg. Ht.

Tub/Shwr.

Bath

Breakfast
12-0 x 7-2
9'-0" Clg. Ht.

Raised Bar

DW

Laundry

Kitchen
12-0 x 10-4

P

R

Raised Bar

Bath

Tub/Shwr.

Hall

Living Room
17-6 x 12-10
(CLEAR)
9'-0" Clg. Ht.

Bedroom 2
11-6 x 13-0
9'-0" Clg. Ht.

Front Porch
17-10 x 5-0

© Copyright by designer/architect

Plan #M07-008D-0160

Leisure Living With Interior Surprise

1,354 total square feet of living area

2 bedrooms, 1 bath

Crawl space foundation

Special features

Soaring ceilings highlight the kitchen, living and dining areas creating dramatic excitement

A spectacular large deck surrounds the front and both sides of the home

An impressive U-shaped kitchen has a wrap-around breakfast bar and shares fantastic views with both the first and second floors through an awesome wall of glass

Two bedrooms with a bath, a sleeping loft and second floor balcony overlooking the living area complete the home

Price Code A

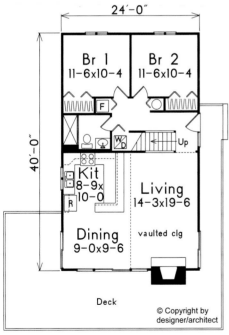

First Floor
960 sq. ft.

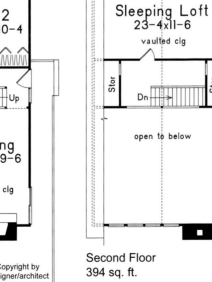

Second Floor
394 sq. ft.

To order this plan, visit the *Menards* Building Materials Desk or visit *www.Menards.com*.

209

Plan #M07-007D-0161

Earth Berm Home With Style

1,480 total square feet of living area

2 bedrooms, 2 baths

2-car garage

Slab foundation

Special features

Energy efficient home with 2" x 6" exterior walls

This home has great looks and lots of space

Nestled in a hillside with only one exposed exterior wall, this home offers efficiency, protection and affordability

The triple patio doors with an arched transom bathe the living room with sunlight

The kitchen features a snack bar open to the living room, large built-in pantry and adjoins a spacious dining room

Price Code A

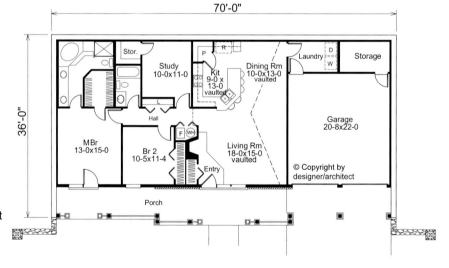

© Copyright by designer/architect

Rear View

To order this plan, visit the Menards Building Materials Desk or visit www.Menards.com.

Plan #M07-007D-0114

Gracious Living On A Small Lot

1,671 total square feet of living area

3 bedrooms, 2 1/2 baths

2-car garage

Basement foundation

Special features

Triple gables and a stone facade create great curb appeal

The two-story entry with hallway leads to a spacious family room, dining area with bay window and U-shaped kitchen

The second floor features a large master bedroom with luxury bath, huge walk-in closet, overlook to entry and two secondary bedrooms with hall bath

Price Code B

First Floor
680 sq. ft.

Second Floor
991 sq. ft.

© Copyright by designer/architect

Rear View

To order this plan, visit the Menards Building Materials Desk or visit www.Menards.com.

211

Plan #M07-058D-0038

Open Floor Plan
With Extra Amenities

1,680 total square feet of living area

3 bedrooms, 2 1/2 baths

2-car garage

Basement foundation

Special features

This home offers a compact and efficient layout in an affordable package

The second floor has three bedrooms all with oversized closets

All bedrooms are located on the second floor for privacy

Price Code B

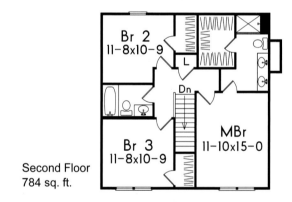

Second Floor
784 sq. ft.

Br 2
11-8x10-9

Br 3
11-8x10-9

MBr
11-10x15-0

L

Dn

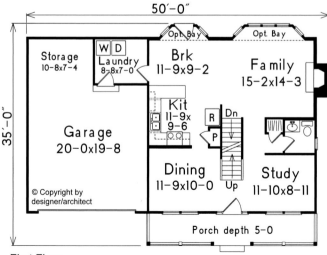

50'-0"

35'-0"

Opt. Bay   Opt. Bay

Storage
10-8x7-4

W D

Laundry
8-8x7-0

Brk
11-9x9-2

Family
15-2x14-3

Kit
11-9x 9-6

Garage
20-0x19-8

R

Dn

P

© Copyright by
designer/architect

Dining
11-9x10-0

Up

Study
11-10x8-11

Porch depth 5-0

First Floor
896 sq. ft.

Rear View

To order this plan, visit the **Menards** Building Materials Desk or visit www.Menards.com.

Plan #M07-008D-0121

Economize Without Sacrifice

960 total square feet of living area

3 bedrooms, 1 bath

Basement foundation, drawings also include crawl space and slab foundations

Special features

This home's attractive appearance adds to any neighborhood

A nice-sized living room leads to an informal family area with eat-in L-shaped kitchen, access to rear yard and basement space

Three bedrooms with lots of closet space and a convenient hall bath complete the home

Price Code AA

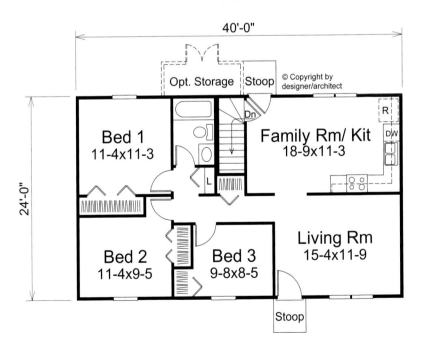

40'-0"

24'-0"

Opt. Storage | Stoop

© Copyright by designer/architect

Dn

Bed 1
11-4x11-3

Family Rm/ Kit
18-9x11-3

R

DW

L

Bed 2
11-4x9-5

Bed 3
9-8x8-5

Living Rm
15-4x11-9

Stoop

MENARDS

Plan #M07-013L-0011

Appealing Charming Porch

1,643 total square feet of living area

3 bedrooms, 2 1/2 baths

2-car drive under side entry garage

Basement or crawl space foundation, please specify when ordering

Special features

The first floor master bedroom has a private bath, walk-in closet and easy access to the laundry closet

The comfortable family room features a vaulted ceiling and a cozy fireplace

Two bedrooms on the second floor share a bath

Price Code C

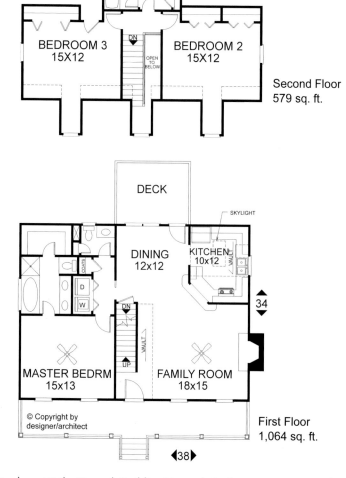

STORAGE

BEDROOM 3
15X12

DN
OPEN
TO
BELOW

BEDROOM 2
15X12

Second Floor
579 sq. ft.

DECK

SKYLIGHT

DINING
12x12

KITCHEN
10x12

VAULT

34

COATS

D

W

DN

VAULT

UP

MASTER BEDRM
15x13

FAMILY ROOM
18x15

© Copyright by
designer/architect

First Floor
1,064 sq. ft.

38

Plan #M07-024L-0044

Peaceful Country Design

1,802 total square feet of living area

3 bedrooms, 2 1/2 baths

2-car side entry garage

Slab or crawl space foundation, please specify when ordering

Special features

The secluded master bedroom includes a private master bath and large walk-in closet

The efficient kitchen easily serves the dining room and bayed breakfast area

The spacious secondary bedrooms enjoy walk-in closets and share the second floor bath

Price Code C

First Floor Plan:

Width: 42'-10"
Depth: 69'-8"

Garage
19'-2" X 23'-8"

Stor.
Cov. Porch

Patio

© Copyright by designer/architect

Utility

Living
20' X 12'-6"

Breakfast
13' X 8'-8"

Bath

Ba.

Kitchen
11' X 10'

Master Bedroom
13' X 16'

Foyer

Dining
11' X 11'-6"

Porch

First Floor
1,185 sq. ft.

Second Floor Plan:

Bath

Bedroom #2
13' X 13'

Bedroom #3
14'-6" X 13'

Second Floor
617 sq. ft.

Pleasant Hill

MENARDS

Plan #M07-024L-0047

Lavish Coastal Retreat

2,205 total square feet of living area

3 bedrooms, 2 baths

2-car drive under carport

Pier foundation

Special features

The double-door entry opens to the spacious two-story living/dining area and kitchen with unique center island

Two secondary bedrooms are secluded from the living areas and enjoy walk-in closets and a shared bath

The master bedroom enjoys a deluxe bath and private balcony

Price Code C

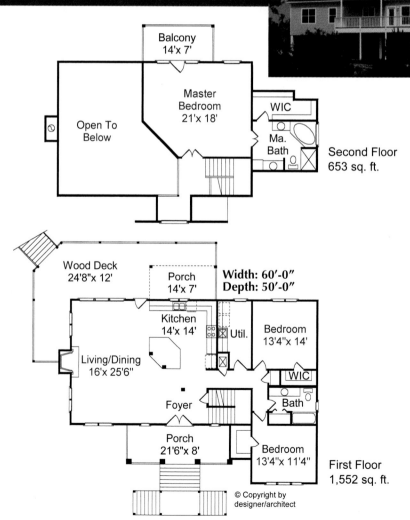

Balcony
14'x 7'

Master
Bedroom
21'x 18'

Open To
Below

WIC

Ma.
Bath

Second Floor
653 sq. ft.

Wood Deck
24'8"x 12'

Porch
14'x 7'

Width: 60'-0"
Depth: 50'-0"

Kitchen
14'x 14'

Util.

Bedroom
13'4"x 14'

Living/Dining
16'x 25'6"

WIC

Foyer

Bath

Porch
21'6"x 8'

Bedroom
13'4"x 11'4"

First Floor
1,552 sq. ft.

© Copyright by
designer/architect

Plan #M07-008D-0148

Corner Window Wall Dominates Design

784 total square feet of living area

3 bedrooms, 1 bath

Pier foundation

Special features

Outdoor relaxation will be enjoyed with this home's huge wrap-around wood deck

Upon entering the spacious living area, a cozy free-standing fireplace, sloped ceiling and corner window wall catch the eye

The charming kitchen features a pass-through peninsula to the dining area

Price Code AAA

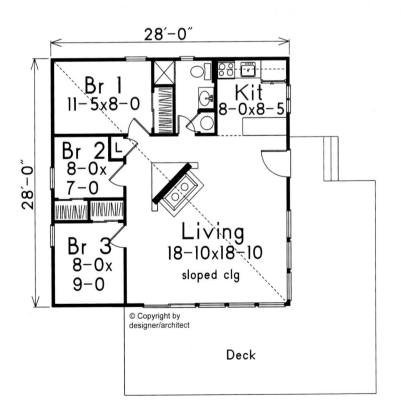

28'-0"

28'-0"

Br 1
11-5x8-0

Kit
8-0x8-5

Br 2 L
8-0x
7-0

Living
18-10x18-10
sloped clg

Br 3
8-0x
9-0

© Copyright by designer/architect

Deck

To order this plan, visit the Menards Building Materials Desk or visit www.Menards.com.

217

Plan #M07-007D-0140

Bright And Airy Country Design

1,591 total square feet of living area

3 bedrooms, 2 baths

2-car side entry garage

Basement foundation

Special features

Spacious porches and a patio provide outdoor enjoyment

The large entry leads to a cheery kitchen and breakfast area that welcomes the sun through a wide array of windows

The great room features a vaulted ceiling, corner fireplace, wet bar and access to the rear patio

Double walk-in closets, private porch and a luxury bath are special highlights of the vaulted master bedroom suite

Price Code B

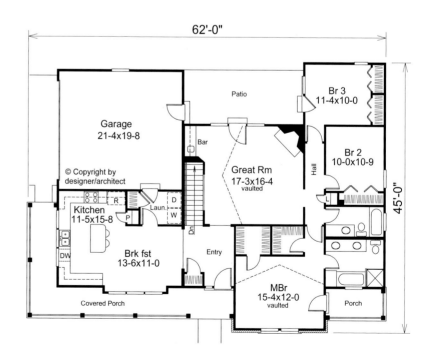

62'-0"

Garage
21-4x19-8

© Copyright by designer/architect

Patio

Br 3
11-4x10-0

Bar

Great Rm
17-3x16-4
vaulted

Br 2
10-0x10-9

Hall

Kitchen
11-5x15-8

Laun.
R
P
D
W

Brk fst
13-6x11-0

Entry

Covered Porch

MBr
15-4x12-0
vaulted

Porch

45'-0"

Rear View

To order this plan, visit the *Menards Building Materials Desk* or visit www.Menards.com.

Plan #M07-007D-0110

Country Charm For A Small Lot

1,169 total square feet of living area

3 bedrooms, 2 baths

1-car garage

Basement foundation

Special features

This home's front facade features a distinctive country appeal

The living room enjoys a wood-burning fireplace and pass-through to the kitchen

A stylish U-shaped kitchen offers an abundance of cabinet and counterspace with a view to the living room

A large walk-in closet, access to the rear patio, and a private bath are some of the many features of the master bedroom

Price Code AA

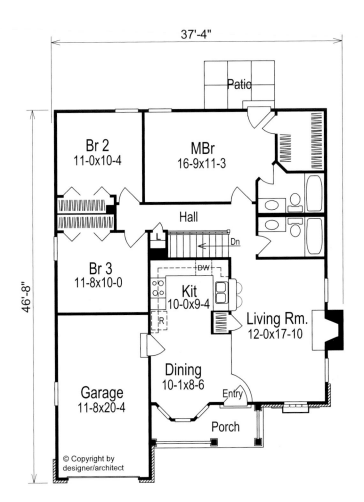

Rear View

Andrew

Plan #M07-013L-0048

Triple Arch Entryway

2,071 total square feet of living area

3 bedrooms, 2 1/2 baths

3-car side entry garage

Basement, slab or crawl space foundation, please specify when ordering

Special features

The entryway dramatically opens to the family room with a high ceiling

The connected screened porch and deck are perfect for outdoor entertaining

The kitchen has easy access to the breakfast area and dining room

The spacious master suite has a cozy sitting room attached

The optional second floor has an additional 434 square feet of living area

Price Code C

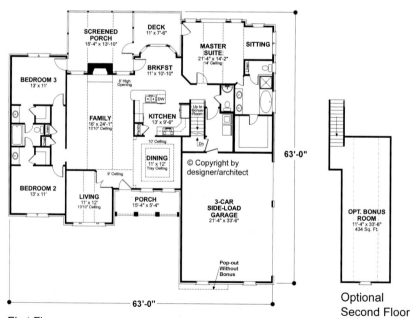

First Floor
2,071 sq. ft.

Optional
Second Floor

Plan #M07-045D-0017

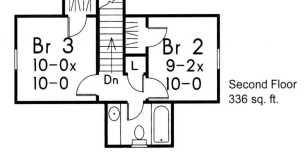

Second Floor
336 sq. ft.

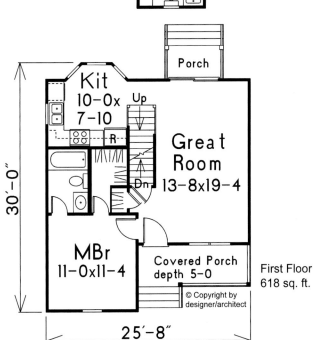

First Floor
618 sq. ft.

© Copyright by designer/architect

Dormer And Covered Porch Add To Country Charm

954 total square feet of living area

3 bedrooms, 2 baths

Basement foundation

Special features

The kitchen has a cozy bayed eating area

The master bedroom has a walk-in closet and private bath

The great room has access to the back porch

The convenient coat closet is located near the front entry

Price Code AA

Rear View

To order this plan, visit the *Menards* Building Materials Desk or visit www.Menards.com.

221

Plan #M07-001D-0086

Open Living/Dining Area

1,154 total square feet of living area

3 bedrooms, 1 1/2 baths

Crawl space foundation, drawings also include slab foundation

Special features

The U-shaped kitchen features a large breakfast bar and handy laundry area

The private second floor bedrooms share a half bath

The large living/dining area opens to the deck

Price Code AA

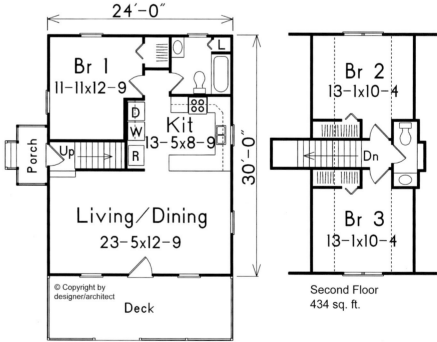

First Floor
720 sq. ft.

24'-0"

30'-0"

Br 1
11-11x12-9

Kit
13-5x8-9

Living/Dining
23-5x12-9

Porch

Up

D
W
R

© Copyright by designer/architect

Deck

Second Floor
434 sq. ft.

Br 2
13-1x10-4

Br 3
13-1x10-4

Dn

Rear View

To order this plan, visit the Menards Building Materials Desk or visit www.Menards.com.

Plan #M07-039L-0002

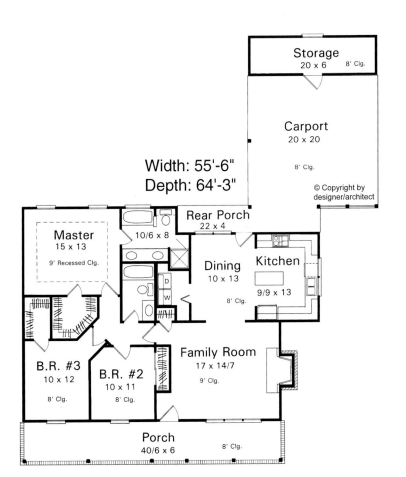

Width: 55'-6"
Depth: 64'-3"

© Copyright by designer/architect

Carport With Storage

1,333 total square feet of living area

3 bedrooms, 2 baths

2-car carport

Slab or crawl space foundation, please specify when ordering

Special features

Country charm with a covered front porch prevails with this home

The dining area looks into the family room with fireplace

The master suite has a walk-in closet and private bath

Price Code A

To order this plan, visit the Menards Building Materials Desk or visit www.Menards.com.

223